# THE EPIC LIFE

## Revelation, Resistance, and Revival

Timothy Floyd

FIDELIS
PUBLISHING

FIDELIS PUBLISHING®

ISBN: 9781956454819
ISBN (eBook): 9781956454826

THE EPIC LIFE
Revelation, Resistance, and Revival

© 2024 Timothy Floyd

Cover Design by Diana Lawrence
Interior Design by Xcel Graphic
Edited by Amanda Varian
Cover painting: *San Juan Evangelista en la isla de Patmos*
by Pedro Orrente (1580–1645)

Order at www.faithfultext.com for a significant discount. Email info@fidelispublishing.com to inquire about bulk purchase discounts.

Manufactured in the United States of America

10 9 8 7 6 5 4 3 2 1

Fidelis Publishing, LLC
Winchester, VA • Nashville, TN
fidelispublishing.com

*To Jonnel*

*Who surprises me with joy every day*
*And has for years encouraged me to put these*
*ideas in writing.*

# CONTENTS

# INTRODUCTION

# A BIT PART IN AN EPIC DRAMA

> *"I wish it need not have happened in my time," said Frodo.*
> *"So do I," said Gandalf, "and so do all who live to see such times.*
> *But that is not for them to decide. All we have to decide is what*
> *to do with the time that is given to us."*
> —*The Fellowship of the Ring*, J. R. R. Tolkien

Have you noticed how often the word *unprecedented* comes up whenever people talk about the politics or cultural fashions of the present age? The government's use of technology to censor or shut down free speech feels unprecedented. Seeing beloved historical figures slandered and finally canceled for conventional ideas that became unfashionable fifteen minutes ago must surely be unprecedented. It's an absolutely unprecedented moment when toddlers are encouraged to question their gender and twelve-year-olds can undergo sex-reassignment surgery in response to typical adolescent mood swings and insecurities.

Ironically, the unparalleled cultural insanity evolving before our eyes in this "brave, new world" most frequently calls to mind two very familiar books, both of them old and dusty. The first is *1984* written by George Orwell in 1949. For Orwell's hero, Winston Smith, life was a daily struggle in a world where "Big Brother is watching you." The Ministry of Truth rewrote and repackaged yesterday's news to conform history to the Party's agenda. Thought police violently enforced the authorized narrative of the week. And the two-way telescreens in every living room endlessly regurgitated mind-numbing slogans to live by: "War is Peace. Freedom is Slavery. Ignorance is Strength."

The other book that comes to mind almost every week is even more ancient. The ideas and images of John's Revelation, the closing book of the Bible, are recalled and confirmed on a daily basis. Granted, the book is so widely regarded as mind-boggling it doesn't get much respect anymore, but it surely gets a lot of traction.

Many people think of the mark of the beast coming into play through social credit scores and digital currency. A few also suppose John anticipates satellite technology when he describes unfolding events seen in real time by everyone on earth. But let me assure you, the big picture in Revelation is much, much bigger than that.

- John's vision foresees the return of absolute government, the all-powerful regime that insists paying taxes and obeying the law are not nearly enough. You must change the way you think and conform to politically correct ideas. Silence is violence.
- He points to a future where the whole world will rage against a relatively microscopic strip of land called Israel. In 2023, most were taken by surprise when Hamas invaded Israel with a wave of murder, rape, and kidnapping. For many, it was even more surprising to see hatred of the Jews instantly erupt around the globe and America's college campuses. John told us things like this were in the wind.

- The USA is never mentioned in Revelation, but the role of decadent American culture in undermining, corrupting, and secularizing the sensibilities of nations around the world is clearly, unmistakably foreshadowed.

How did so many Christians and commentators miss that? Here's how. The mere suggestion of reading through Revelation—this prophetically accurate survival guide for believers—causes most churchgoers to roll their eyes, groan, and throw up their hands. We've been programmed to believe John's vision requires details and knowledge we don't have. The prevailing theory of Revelation insists it's all about some unlucky future generation destined for unprecedented horrors. Another view argues John is telling the story of a historic group of Christians from the Roman Empire in the first century. In other words, we've had it drummed into our heads that whatever happens in the final book of the Bible is either about the distant future or the ancient past. If the past is unfamiliar, and the future is unknowable, what's the point of even going there?

Here's the good news: Revelation is about you and me and this unsettling moment where we currently find ourselves. It explains some of the forces and events that make this twenty-first-century storm seem so confusing and even frightening. John writes about seven principles that will keep us moving boldly into challenging headwinds. And you don't need to be a history scholar, a futurist, or a CIA analyst to decipher the mysterious images of his vision from Patmos. The only tool you'll need is one you already have: your Bible.

Another over-used word in our post-modern lexicon is "apocalyptic." Perhaps you've noticed every threat earns that moniker these days. Climate change is apocalyptic. Pandemics are apocalyptic. Bombs, earthquakes, and CAT-5 hurricanes all threaten to bring the apocalypse.

If this all seems a bit unnerving, read Revelation. John completely understands the apocalypse. He gave us that word for unveiling—the revelation of something hidden. It's the Greek title of the last book in the Bible, which explains why such a technical term still resonates in the West. We would all benefit from less white noise from social media influencers and more counsel from people with divine wisdom and deep life experience. Selah.

You and I stand watch in a dark moment when our beloved "Land of the Free" is in decline. Every institution has been infected with a deadly mind virus: the courts, education, industry, entertainment, sports, science, and even the church. Materialism, sexual decadence, and woke religion have run amok across the entire national landscape. But don't be fooled. This is not a political campaign or a silly culture war. This is a spiritual war.

J. R. R. Tolkien's words are as true now as ever. We don't get to choose the times in which we live. Our only choice is how we can respond courageously to the time given us. Revelation has strengthened my decision-making for decades. I hope John's vision will capture your imagination and your heart as well.

## Life on an Eternal Scale

"They will make war on the Lamb, and the
Lamb will conquer them, for he is Lord of lords
and King of kings, and those with him are called
and chosen and faithful." (Rev. 17:14)

For those of us who follow Christ, the sacrifices made by martyrs and heroes of the distant past should make perfect sense. Yes, it must have been brutal standing up to oppressive governments and rival religions, but the kingdom of God is worth it. Right? We imagine how we would have been fully engaged had we been invited to walk with Jesus against all odds. We glibly mock Simon Peter for denying his friendship with Christ when he feared he might be arrested. And whenever we read historical accounts of Christians dying for their faith in the Roman Colosseum or risking life and limb to own an English Bible in 1525, we assure ourselves we would have stood with the faithful.

In fact, as recently as 2020, all U.S. churches were forbidden to meet for worship by government decrees, some for a few months and others much longer, but there was no united resistance from believers. When worship was classified "non-essential," there was scarcely a peep from the saints. Even when "essential businesses" like supermarkets, big box stores, and liquor stores remained open; and Black Lives Matter protestors were encouraged by the same politicians to gather en masse, march without wearing paper masks, and even riot, most churches in the United States meekly bowed the knee, completely shut out. Our rationale was not faith, but fear: fear of punishment, fear of men, or fear of a virus.

Compare our response to that of the early church. When the Antonine Plague struck the Roman Empire in AD 190, the contagion killed 20 percent of the population. The spread of the infection was so rampant that many fled the cities, carrying the disease with them. Others tossed family members into the streets at the first sign of the infection, hoping to save themselves. Rather than cowering at home, sheltering in place, Roman Christians not only cared for their own sick relatives but went into the streets to rescue strangers abandoned to die.

Historians conclude this was one of the factors in the rapid spread of the gospel throughout the pagan Roman Empire. Desperate pagans recognized the church was about much more than pie in the sky and hymn singing. The people who called themselves Christians exemplified sacrificial love and indestructible joy. Most amazing of all, they weren't afraid to die. In stark contrast to that historic outcome, it's apparent to everyone in the present day the COVID-19 pandemic weakened most U.S. churches and finished others off completely.

Faced with a new threat, we accepted political assurances that this was in the national interest, and necessary for the greater good. But first-century Romans heard the same rationale when they were commanded to worship Caesar with a pinch of incense or else. "It's how we keep the empire unified and strong," the emperors and their lackeys insisted. But the saints of Rome were not half-hearted or fearful. "We'd rather die," they replied. And quite a few of them did.

In 1525, when translating the Bible into English was a capital crime, English churches were reassured that hunting down Bible translators and their supporters was in the national interest. If ordinary, uneducated people were suddenly able to read God's Word in their own tongue, they would misunderstand the teachings so badly that there would soon be deadly divisions in the church and utter confusion across the land. William Tyndale, a brilliant scholar who spoke seven languages, left his homeland to spend years translating the New Testament while in hiding. He trusted a source of authority higher than corrupt kings and governors. His outlawed translation of the Word spread like wildfire.

The Bible was not written to us, but it was written for us. That's why we should examine ourselves when Jesus rebukes his religious listeners, "You know how to interpret the appearance of the sky, but you cannot interpret the signs of the times" (Matt. 16:3). Many of us who consider ourselves A-students in worship might be shocked to find we have completely failed in Bible application. We know what Shadrach, Meshach, and Abednego told the king of Babylon, but have no idea what we should say to the confused people around us in offices and on golf courses.

The bad news is the Beast has arisen again to wreak havoc and take prisoners. The good news is Jesus Christ is on the throne and has called up the Armies of Light. That's the message of an earth-shaking book called Revelation, "The Unveiling." I want to help you dig into this book, the most controversial in the Bible. As we reap the insights of John's Revelation, God will equip us to stand tall even as darkness descends all about us.

Today's headlines are grim, but life doesn't have to seem bleak. Go back in your mind to the last time you enjoyed an epic movie and relive that familiar experience for a moment. You sit there spellbound. There is agony and warfare. Heroes and warriors battle against overwhelming odds, and many succumb to a noble death. Beyond all that pain and self-sacrifice, your heart swells within you as the musical score begins to rise. Something resonates deep in your core, but it's more than grand music, great faces, and realistic computer-generated images. You are captivated because the story has tapped into the ancient, shared wisdom of your soul telling you this is absolute truth and timeless reality.

Quality of life is real, but it only emerges when we comprehend there's a kingdom infinitely more momentous and beautiful than our paltry existence, our impulses and appetites, and a handful of possessions. Greatness happens when the price I am willing to pay for that destiny is bigger than everything I own, everything I am. That's when life becomes epic.

Revelation is the climax and conclusion of the only book that has ever turned the world upside down and continues to transform people and nations. Through sixty-five books of flawed heroes, thrilling stories, and timeless ideas, the Bible builds upon interlocking narratives and a singular message. Then Revelation caps off that magnum opus with jolting images of courageous living on a doomed planet.

It's too bad so many have dismissed this closing book of the Bible as a forbidden jungle of complex timetables, pointless tragedies, and unrelenting negativity. This is the book that ties together all those profound narratives and principles advanced throughout Scripture. The tree of life disappears early in Genesis but turns up again in Revelation. Texts in Psalms and Romans teach us not to seek revenge against those who mistreat us but to trust God to avenge injustice. Revelation captures how that looks. Acts describes the Lord's ascent to heaven, but Revelation describes his return to earth.

Let's spend a few days walking through Revelation together. This travel guide, *The Epic Life*, does not move through John's message in a linear manner the way most books on the subject do. Rather than interpreting everything for you, I want to equip you to experience the pinnacle of Scripture for yourself. Most commentaries on this subject leave their readers interested but still baffled. I want to send you away confident and motivated.

Here's what you can expect from this book. The first three chapters unpack the three most basic tools you'll need to unlock John's apocalypse. Chapters 4 through 8 introduce the cast and storyline, equipping you to interpret them accurately. In chapters 9 through 11, you'll learn the seven principles we must build into our lives and attitudes. And finally, chapter 12 unpacks the political, spiritual, and social chaos of the present era, highlighting the biblical ways we must respond.

John's Revelation will help you take stock of your allegiance to Christ and reallocate how you invest your most valuable resource, your time. As you will soon discover, it's a vision given to us for times like these.

CHAPTER ONE

# THE DRAGON'S LAIR

*"In this year there were immense flashes of lightning,*
*and fiery dragons in the air, and a little after that the raiding*
*of heathen men destroyed God's church in Lindisfarne."*
—Anglo-Saxon Chronicle, AD 793

The Great Tribulation is not a hyperspace zombie apocalypse on steroids reserved for some unlucky future generation. If that news strikes you as shocking, just think logically for a moment. What looming terrors inflicted by laser beams or futuristic high-tech weapons could ever be any more terrifying or agonizing than the gruesome torture, slaughter, and mutilation inflicted on the Irish monks of Lindisfarne in the eighth century AD when the first blood-thirsty Vikings arrived in their long boats? Would you rather be evaporated by a laser beam or watch your comrades tortured with axes, knives, and fire before you are finally disemboweled and decapitated?

It was great tribulation that fell upon those unsuspecting saints of Ireland, and it felt remarkably like the images they envisioned reading John's Revelation. Alien craft came slicing through dark waters, the heads of snarling dragons carved into every prow, rising suddenly from the mist. Violent, well-armed berserkers roared, shrieking in a foreign tongue as they charged. Then came the unthinkable, beyond their nightmares or wildest imaginations.

This sort of trial by fire has been shared by believers somewhere around the world in every generation since the cross, and with each new outbreak the promises of Revelation have resonated with the broken hearts of the saints. Tertullian explained how the kingdom of God advances in the face of persecution: "The blood of the martyrs is the seed of the church." So it was that the Viking terror ended just about two centuries later after most of the Norse tribes renounced Odin and converted to Christianity. It certainly wasn't painless, but it wasn't pointless either.

## What's a Picture Worth?

> The revelation of Jesus Christ, which God gave him to show to his servants the things that must soon take place. He made it known by sending his angel to his servant John. (Rev. 1:1)

The message of Revelation has been delivered to you and me in writing, but it was originally given to John in pictures. The Lord showed his scarred, aging servant a vision of events that would soon take place. Some things like the return of Christ would wait further down the road, but many things envisioned by John were in the wings or already unfolding. Significantly, John recalls an angel "made it known." That phrase is a translation of the Greek word *semaino*, which means "to reveal something in signs or symbols." The KJV uses the word "signified."

Revelation self-describes as a collection of signs shown to John by a messenger from heaven. That's not a personal interpretation. It's how the author explains what we are reading. His guidance will help us digest the visual feast we're about to be served.

Literalists worry this reduces Revelation to allegory, watering down the message, but that defies both the text and common sense. Figurative language does not imply an event isn't real or significant. The old idea "a picture is worth a thousand words" still resonates today because images generally communicate more vividly than adjectives. Would you rather arrive at the airport with a photo of the stranger you're supposed to pick up or a verbal description?

Like all beloved literature, Scripture abounds with metaphor, simile, and hyperbole. Our heavenly Father is the master communicator, and his message is profound. He was speaking figuratively when he spoke of the Israelites tying his commandments to their hands and wearing them on their foreheads (Deut. 6:8). Some Jews still take this literally, wearing tiny boxes on their hands and heads, but we know the idea was metaphorical because Jesus never wore such a device or recommended the practice. Rather, God desired his people to take his words to heart, reflecting them in their thinking as well as their actions. In Psalm 23, David compared himself to a sheep, although he didn't eat in green pastures and wasn't frightened of moving waters. The truth is bigger than all that. And of course, Jesus sometimes referred to himself as a shepherd. The fact that he was a carpenter by trade did not suggest he was either dishonest or unserious.

When the Anglo-Saxon historian of AD 793 envisioned lightning flashes and fiery dragons heralding the arrival of Viking berserkers, he captured for us the terror and the overwhelming chaos of an event that changed ancient history. He helped us relate a crisis from the distant past to our present reality. We understand more, not less. That's why the Lord's vision for John is heavily laden with signs and figurative language. Like the apostle, we need to grapple with the full impact of his prophecy because something profound is at stake.

In Revelation 1:8, for example, Christ identifies himself as the Alpha and the Omega. Those are letters in the Greek alphabet, most notably the first and the last. They tell us Christ is the creator, the person who spoke the cosmos into being. He is also the judge, the one who will one day destroy the earth and initiate the transition to eternity. On one hand, this explains his authority to shape our lives, to give us commandments, and to hold us accountable for what we do with the resources he's provided. On the other hand, whenever God's people walk through the valley of the shadow, it comforts us to know the author and judge of all creation is walking with us. Figurative language helps us get the point.

God also relies on imagery when he reveals Christ, the Son of Man, garbed in white and gold attire, with hair as white as wool and eyes like flames (1:12–16). Of course, this has to be Jesus. He identifies himself as the Son of Man, the first and the last, and the only person who ever died to be resurrected never to die again. But when did he ever look like this? The use of simile here tells us about his wisdom, his ability to see all and judge rightly, his indestructibility, and his authority. As Christ's best friend, John has spent months with the Lord on the road, but he faints, utterly collapsing to the ground when he sees Christ like this. The Prince of Peace we love so much is also our Eternal God, the Lord of Justice. This image of Jesus Christ helps us appreciate Paul's guidance to "work out your own salvation with fear and trembling" (Philippians 2:12).

Making the most of Revelation means watching a vision narrated by John and carefully defining what each picture represents. One moment we meet a Jesus with white hair, fiery eyes, and metallic feet. A few pages later, he's a lamb on a throne. Neither image is literal, but each one reveals important truths about the Son of God. So, when he begins to remove the seven seals and loose the scroll containing God's final plan for the earth, we know the seals and the scroll are signs as well. Those archaic objects will teach us about present-day forces and a final destiny that are very real indeed.

Read slowly. You won't find any supersonic aircraft or hellfire missiles rocketing through the air in these pages, but you will find an explanation of why your world is suddenly so hateful, so pagan, so willing to believe lies and demand that everyone must accept them as true. You'll discover why we suddenly have an epidemic known as Rapid Onset Gender Dysphoria; a condition among girls that didn't exist twenty years ago. If you want to see F-16s, you can always go to an airshow. But if you want truth about where the world is headed, turn to John's Revelation. And read slowly.

## Secrets of an Epic Life

Blessed is the one who reads aloud the words of this prophecy, and blessed are those who hear, and who keep what is written in it, for the time is near. (Rev. 1:3)

John's Revelation was not delivered to us as a crystal ball or a psychic doorway to facts and details of some sordid future. It was the Lord who cautioned us, "Therefore do not be anxious about tomorrow, for tomorrow will be anxious for itself" (Matt. 6:34). The complexities of the future rest completely in God's hands. It's the decisions of today that are left to us. The constant admonition of the New Testament is we should live each day and every hour as though the Lord's return might come at any moment. It could happen.

The purpose of John's vision is stated unambiguously here in the opening verses of his letter. There are blessings to be reaped by those who live this day and every day in a particular manner. "Blessed are those who hear, and who keep what is written in it, for the time is near." John wants to be instructive rather than predictive. There's little we can do to derail most future tragedies, but there are specific things we can do today to be prepared for whatever comes down the pike. Some attitudes and disciplines bring blessings today and tomorrow.

Throughout the New Testament, blessedness denotes happiness. Who doesn't want to enjoy some tranquility—especially when you're facing adversity and opposition? It was actually this promise that motivated me to investigate Revelation for myself nearly three decades ago. I heard great pastors expound the earthshaking events of John's vision and read popular books about the nuclear war, laser-guided missiles, and a Soviet invasion John foresaw. But nobody ever called my attention to principles that would bring God's blessing to me. What was I supposed to be keeping, anyway? Fundamentally, what sets the people of God apart before they are dragged off to the Roman Colosseum and after they step into the arena to face the lions?

John was very familiar with the heroes of Hebrews 11, those Old Testament saints who raised the bar for faith, even in the face of oppression, persecution, and martyrdom. Some like Noah, Abraham, and Moses are cited by name. Many others are simply celebrated as a group for their refusal to cave. "They were stoned, they were sawn in two, they were killed with the sword. They went about in skins of sheep and goats, destitute, afflicted, mistreated—of whom the world was not worthy" (Heb. 11:37–38).

These holy champions are remembered for loving God and living out the truth even when the cost seemed exorbitant. What can we draw from their courageous examples for use in our own lives? That is the core of John's vision. His apocalypse or unveiling is structured around seven churches. As we shall see, those churches are real, but the seven of them are arrayed figuratively to coach and encourage suffering saints. The letters to those churches remind us of the seven best practices taught by God and cultivated by people of faith for centuries. Everything else in the vision—all the characters and catastrophes—reiterates the necessity of those seven character qualities. John's Revelation imposes a vision of God's certain judgment upon the earth to teach us the kind of people we should be.

If that sounds familiar, it should. Another apostle named Simon Peter concluded his second and final epistle in a remarkably similar fashion. After describing how the heavenly bodies will ultimately be burned up as the earth is melted down, he raises the obvious question: "Since all these things are thus to be dissolved, what sort of people ought you to be . . . ?" (2 Pet. 3:11).

## God Paints with Dark Colors

> I, John, your brother and partner in tribulation
> and the kingdom and the patient endurance that
> are in Jesus, was on the island called Patmos on
> account of the word of God and the testimony of
> Jesus. (Rev. 1:9)

John's original audience was likely not thinking about blood-thirsty Norsemen coming ashore in longboats eight centuries in the future when they heard John's message read aloud. In the Roman world of AD 90, terror and violence descended from the highest levels of government: Caesar. Unlike earlier emperors who realized emperor worship was a political calculation, Domitian sincerely believed he was divine. Fueled by delusions of divinity and unchecked ambition, he was more than willing to inflict misery and death on anyone who challenged him: disloyal relatives, stubborn senators, careless envoys, and certainly those annoying Christians who refused to bow to him. Historians recall his final years as a reign of terror.

The last surviving apostle writes from a small island where enemies of the state were exiled. John had run afoul of the emperor when his reputation as a spiritual leader reached the royal palace. Refusing to worship as required by law, he was sentenced to be boiled in oil. When he miraculously survived that ordeal, he was banished to the prison isle. We can only imagine the scars and health complications that must have accompanied him to such a primitive place after his personal trial by fire.

He identifies himself as a brother in tribulation, in the kingdom, and in patient endurance. He is not surprised by opposition to the faith. Christ prepared his disciples for persecution early in their time together (Matt. 10:16–19). Even so, the basic truths of the gospel must be taught and retaught to each new generation of saints. Otherwise, young believers grow up with rosy optimism, unprepared for the onslaught of the Dragon and his forces. In a world enflamed by our sinful nature, opposition to God has always been the rule, not the exception.

Many of us here in the twenty-first century imagine the gospel as a guarantee of stress-free living and financial prosperity, but the Bible never even hints at heaven on earth. In Genesis, the people of Israel struggle to survive the same famine afflicting their pagan neighbors. When their deliverance finally dawns, it arrives with an exemplary young Hebrew named Joseph who ascends to power in Egypt after thirteen long years of injustice, oppression, and imprisonment. A few pages later, a new pharaoh will feel so threatened by the growing population of Jews that he will reduce their lives to bitter slavery, hoping to break their very will to live. History will require a man like Moses to lead them to freedom, but he must spend forty years in the blistering Sinai wilderness before he will be equipped to lead his people out of Egypt and through the desert to the Land of Promise. That's just the first two books of the Bible.

God's Word reminds us time and again that distress and personal trial are not random interruptions to the life of faith: *they are the point of it.* It is in facing the fires of adversity and uncertainty that men and women discover the meaning of life, the purpose for being. In the kingdom of God, mountaintop experiences are the exception, mere momentary glimpses of clarity and delight. Struggle and discomfort abound in life. We are not yet in heaven: *this is the wilderness where the most basic survival tool is persistent faith.* And from time to time, only manna enables us to survive.

## Think about It

1. Read Revelation 1 in its entirety. Then slowly read it again.
2. What sort of bad news does John convey in this chapter? What's the good news?
3. Why is it so tempting to imagine cataclysmic meltdowns in the distant future instead of searching the biblical text to identify principles we should practice today?

4. Can you recall a very painful season of adversity in your own life God used to strengthen you, grow your faith, and otherwise bless you?
5. Take another look at Revelation 1:12–18. What literal truths about Jesus Christ are communicated by this symbolic representation?

# CHAPTER TWO

# I'VE SEEN THAT FACE BEFORE

*And the four living creatures, each of them with six wings,*
*are full of eyes all around and within, and day and night they*
*never cease to say, "Holy, holy, holy, is the Lord God Almighty,*
*who was, and is and is to come!"*
—Revelation 4:8

Don't forget about your roots on your way to the sky. You'd be amazed how many idealistic and ambitious people in the West have made that mistake before crashing painfully back to reality. Public debate is awash with voices demanding the influence of Christianity be stripped from every aspect of public life. They imagine themselves as champions of secular virtues like freedom, equality, and love. And they assume those are universal human values that have always been the ideal. Unfortunately, their ignorance is deep.

For most of human history, for example, virtually everyone believed human trafficking was not only natural but necessary. Most slaves might have hated their cruel

bonds, but they would also have hoped for slaves of their
own if only their tribes or nations had been more effective
in warfare and weaponry. Influential Greeks and Romans
like Aristotle, Plato, and Epictetus championed the notion
that some people were fit only for slavery, human tools
born to be ruled by their superiors. It's well-known to
historians that neither Greek nor Roman literature mentioned equality, freedom, or love in any listing of national
virtues. Rather, Jesus Christ is the demonstrable source of
all those lofty virtues so fundamental to Western Civiliza-
tion. At the time he encouraged sharing with the poor,
finding freedom in truth, or treating women with respect,
such ideas were radical and visionary. Our aspirations for
freedom, equality, and love are all rooted in him.

In the same way, the Christian faith finds its roots in
the Judaism of the Old Testament. Ancient blood sacrifices offered year after year in the temple anticipated the
sacrifice of Jesus Christ who would embrace death on
the cross to atone for the sins of humankind once and
for all. The Old Covenant Passover became the heart of
the New Covenant Lord's Supper. Jesus Christ, a Jew,
relied completely on well-known Hebrew prophecies to
confirm his identity as the Messiah. When King Herod
conspired to locate and destroy the newborn king, even
his corrupt aides were aware of the Old Testament promise of the Messiah being born in Bethlehem.

Early in his ministry, Christ cautioned his heady disciples that he had not come to overturn the Law and the
Prophets, but to fulfill them (Matt. 5:17). That instructive
proposition works in two directions. Yes, it means those
mysterious and amazing events of the Old Testament find
their fullest expression in Jesus Christ. It also means stu-
dents of the New Testament can draw profound insights
from the Old. That brings us to the second essential tool
for understanding John's apocalyptic vision.

Every character or figure you encounter in Revelation can first be found in the Old Testament. Surprised? Don't be. Most believers in this generation have never been taught to study the Old Testament for any reason, particularly to unlock the book of Revelation. Instead, the prevailing approaches to the apocalypse encourage the use of imagination. The Beast must be some notorious, global figure like Hitler, a particular Pope, or the current leader of the World Economic Forum. Which one sounds most likely to you? And what does it denote when John envisions the sky rolling up like a scroll? Use your imagination. That sounds just like a thermonuclear explosion being detonated, doesn't it?

Anything is possible, but that interpretative standard has two problems. First, the original apostles and their disciples could have never comprehended any of our recent celebrities or technologies many centuries in their future. The book would have been meaningless to John's original readers. Second, if the only limit on interpretation is my imagination, the final book of the Bible can mean anything and everything. One Protestant reader thinks the Beast sounds a lot like Pope Leo X, who excommunicated Martin Luther, but then there's a Roman Catholic reader who suddenly discovers Martin Luther looks like the beastly villain. You wanna make a wager?

The Old Testament is a much more reliable source for understanding Revelation and the most likely one as well. With that in mind, let's identify some of John's most prominent characters and trace them back to their origins. Check out these references for yourself, but don't get bogged down so early. I'll elaborate on a couple of practical examples in a moment, and then we'll revisit and flesh out many of these characters or images in subsequent chapters.

| Figure in Revelation | Old Testament Source |
|---|---|
| • Son of Man, 1:13 | Daniel 7:9–14 |
| • Glorious Man in a Robe, 1:12–16 | Daniel 10:5–7 |
| • Four Six-Winged Creatures, 4:6–10 | Ezekiel 1:4–14 |
| • The Mysterious Scroll, 5:1 | Daniel 10:10–12:4 |
| • The Lamb, 5:1–7 | Exodus 12:1–11 (John 1:29) |
| • Four Horsemen, 6:1–8 | Zechariah 1:7–11 |
| • Black Sun, Blood Moon, 6:12–14 | Isaiah 13:9–10; Joel 2:10, 31 |
| • Two Witnesses, Olive Trees, 11:1–14 | Zechariah 4:1–14 |
| • Woman with Sun, Moon, Stars, 12:1–4 | Genesis 37:9 |
| • The Beast from the Sea, 13:1–9; 17:7–8 | Daniel 7:7–14, 19–25 |
| • The Mark of the Beast, 13:16–18 | Ezekiel 9:3–8 |
| • Babylon, the Great Harlot, 17:1–8; 18:1–10 | Jeremiah 51:7; Isaiah 51:19 |

## Voices from the Dim, Distant Past

Perhaps they were primitive, those barefoot Hebrew men wearing animal skins, reading and recording divine revelations by torchlight. They certainly weren't ignorant. Hundreds of years after they left the planet, John the apostle saw their visions come to life again. Fast-forward another two millennia and their words and ideas are still consulted by educated men and women working on computers and relying on satellite technology. Such is the economy of God's universe.

The prophets of the Old Testament hold the keys to the divine vision streamed for John on the prison isle called Patmos. There's been quite a debate over the decades about the identity of the four mysterious creatures in the throne room of God (Rev. 4:6–11). John describes an ox, a lion, an eagle, and a man—all covered in eyes and using six wings to move about. Some have insisted the four represent Matthew, Mark, Luke, and John. Others have argued they signify domestic animals, wild animals, flying creatures, and mankind. But for people familiar with the Old Testament, there's nothing to argue about.

The book of Ezekiel opens with a terrifying scene unfolding before the exiled prophet along the Chebar Canal in Babylon. In Ezekiel 1:1–28, the heavens open with lightning and fire and a cloud that gleams like metal. If it sounds like a UFO (UAP in Newspeak), you can relax. Mysterious creatures emerge from the cloud. Amazingly all four bear the likeness of an ox, an eagle, a lion, and a man, and they appear before the throne of God amid flashes of lightning and peals of thunder. John's description is much more concise than the detailed chapter Ezekiel devotes to the figures, but the connection is obvious. And there's no mystery. Ezekiel explains (1:28) that this is the appearance of the likeness of the glory of the Lord. He recalls falling to his face as the voice of God begins to address him.

Like the earth, heaven is filled with the glory of God. His matchless worth and eternal power are reflected by the splendor of creation, the power and intricacy of the Bible, and the surrender of men and women who rise in faith to fulfill the mission of the kingdom of light. No wonder John explains how every time the four creatures give glory and honor to the Creator, the twenty-four

elders in heaven fall down in worship (Rev. 4:9). That
is, of course, what worshippers do. We offer thanks and
praise and adoration for the grace and majesty of God
unfolding all around us.

## A Man Like No Other

> . . . and in the midst of the lampstands one like
> the son of man, clothed with a long robe and
> with a golden sash around his chest. The hairs on
> his head were white, like white wool, like snow.
> His eyes were like a flame of fire. (Rev. 1:13–14)

We unpacked this figurative appearance of Jesus in the
previous chapter. But looking more deeply, we can also
trace this part of John's vision all the way back to the Old
Testament, specifically the book of Daniel. In one vision,
the prophet encounters the Ancient of Days seated on a
fiery throne. "His clothing was white as snow, and the
hair of his head like pure wool" (Dan 7:9). This denotes
God Almighty, the eternal judge served by angels too
numerous to count. Three chapters later, an eternal messenger comes calling on Daniel in a vision. This figure is
described as "a man clothed in linen, with a belt of fine
gold from Uphaz around his waist. His body was like
beryl, his face like the appearance of lightning, his eyes
like flaming torches, his arms and legs like the gleam of
burnished bronze . . ." (10:5–6).

   In Daniel, these beings represent different authorities. One is obviously God. The other seems more like a
messenger, perhaps the angel Gabriel. But in Revelation,
all these eternal qualities of wisdom, power, and divine
intervention are invested in one being: the One and Only,
God's only begotten Son. Here God unveils the Christ,
the singular being who demonstrates the most profound

qualities imaginable. He not only rules in perfect power and reigns with eternal wisdom, but he humbles himself to intervene personally, depicting himself as standing in the very midst of the suffering saints.

In John's vision, we are told the seven lampstands represent the seven churches addressed in the letter (Rev. 1:20). The seven stars are the pastors of those churches. And the risen and reigning Jesus Christ stands at the center of those persecuted congregations, holding their pastors (messengers) in his hand. That's what God wants the church under fire in any age to understand about his commitment to them.

## The Pregnant Woman and the Scarlet Dragon

> And a great sign appeared in heaven: a woman clothed with the sun, with the moon under her feet, and on her head a crown of twelve stars. She was pregnant and was crying out in birth pains and the agony of giving birth. (Rev. 12:1–2)

It doesn't require much imagination to conclude the pregnant woman must denote the Virgin Mary. The text elaborates further that she will give birth to a son who will rule the world. The boy will be caught up with God and his throne, and the new mother will spend three and a half months in the wilderness. We have no record of Mary fleeing into the desert after Jesus was resurrected and ascended to the Father, so what's that all about? If this isn't about Mary, what is God telling us here?

Once again, the Old Testament is a reliable key. In Genesis 37, Joseph shares a couple of dreams with his family, causing his envious stepbrothers to despise him even more. One of those dreams depicts the sun, the

moon, and eleven stars bowing at Joseph's feet. His parents and siblings are offended, knowing intuitively this is
about the entire family of Jacob falling to honor Joseph.
The sun, moon, and eleven stars represent the nuclear
family that will give birth to the people of Israel.

In John's vision, God uses the same image to describe
Judaism, the Old Covenant faith, giving birth to the
church of Jesus Christ, the New Covenant faith. Mary
is surrounded by the celestial elements from Joseph's
vivid dream.

We don't even need Old Testament clues to discover
the identity of the Dragon who pursues her. Only a few
verses later John writes, "And the great dragon was
thrown down, that ancient serpent, who is called the
devil and Satan, the deceiver of the whole world—he was
thrown down to the earth, and his angels were thrown
down with him" (Rev. 12:9).

As you watch the Dragon wreak havoc on the earth,
often by dispatching proxies to do his bidding, remember how the rest of the New Testament describes his role.
Paul calls him "the prince of the power of the air, the
spirit that is now at work in the sons of disobedience"
(Eph. 2:2). Elsewhere, John asserts, "[The] whole world
lies in the power of the evil one" (1 John 5:19). There is
certainty and purpose in our world because God reigns
and advances his purposes with all authority and power.
But Satan, a prince rather than a king, exerts his seductive influence to ensure civil war continues in defiance of
God's administration. Stay tuned. In Revelation, we will
see this problem resolved once and for all.

In this segment of his vision, the battered but not
beaten man of God describes the transition from Moses
to Jesus. Once Judaism gives birth to their Messiah, Jesus
assumes the center stage of history and the Jews retreat

to the sidelines for a while. (Satan will still despise them, however.) Paul describes the same changeover when he writes, "I ask, then, has God rejected his people? By no means! For I myself am an Israelite, a descendant of Abraham, a member of the tribe of Benjamin. God has not rejected his people whom he foreknew" (Rom. 11:1–2). Rather, Paul explains, the Jews have been set aside to open the gates to the Gentiles. However, it's not forever, and in the fullness of time, God will call them back to himself (vv. 1–11).

Take note that a later segment involving the Dragon will also give us clues for understanding the larger vision. John explains the Dragon's seven heads are a figure for the seven hills where the great harlot is seated (Rev. 17:9–13). This confirms for John's generation, the notorious hooker reflected the corrupting spirit of pagan Rome, famous for its seven hills. Then we are told the ten crowns represent ten kings yet to come. The number is figurative, but it tells us the same scheme will play out in generations still to come. This simple detail alerts us that John's vision will speak to divine forces at work, not only in John's world but in generations yet to arise.

Insights like these illustrate why neither a vivid imagination nor a love of science fiction is constructive in understanding Revelation. God drew all the characters and images from the Old Testament to make the vision comprehensible, not mysterious. That's challenging for us, of course, because most of us spend far more time in the last twenty-seven books of the Bible than the first thirty-nine. The New Testament reveals Jesus Christ to us and offers guidance for daily living. The Old Testament explains why the New Covenant is necessary and gives us insight into how it came about. And yes, it unlocks the final book of the Bible as well.

# Think about It

1. Work through the list of figures from Revelation and their Old Testament sources. Can you see obvious connections between the Old Testament figures and the images John describes?
2. Familiar Greek and Roman mythology featured colorful characters, both good and evil, suggesting moral lessons. What are some of the likely reasons God relied upon Old Testament images for the vision rather than those well-known myths?
3. Think about the details in the image of the all-powerful Christ standing among the persecuted churches. Which aspect resonates most powerfully with you?
4. Explain in your own words how the woman with the sun, moon, and stars around her represents Judaism giving birth to Christianity.

# CHAPTER THREE

# HOW HIGH CAN GOD COUNT?

*Then I turned to see the voice that was speaking to me,*
*and on turning I saw seven golden lampstands.*
—Revelation 1:12

The Navy Seals have a mantra, "Second place is first loser." The rest of us may not be quite that demanding, but the number one does hold extra significance for us all. First place means I rose to the top of the heap. It means I have earned some credibility, some glory. Even if an athlete makes it all the way to the world stage of the Olympic games, silver and bronze are okay but can seem forgettable. The real question is who won the gold? Who is number one?

In the minds of the ancient Hebrew people, several numbers had a significance greater than just their mathematical value. Ironically, the number one was not among that elite group. Nevertheless, other numbers with theological significance come into play whenever we begin to read John's Revelation. Integers like three, seven, and a thousand are incorporated time and again throughout, and they are used in several different contexts. For example, the aging apostle includes letters to seven churches he served. No doubt, he impacted far more congregations than that, but in this setting, the idea of seven churches means more than six congregations plus one. When we realize this basic fact, Revelation begins to make more sense.

Many ancient Hebrew numbers also hold a theological value, but let's just consider a few with particular relevance to us. These are the numbers most commonly cited by John in describing his vision in the cave at Patmos.

It will surprise no one that three is the number of God. Our eternal architect and creator expresses himself in three characters: Father, Son, and Holy Spirit. Jonah was in the belly of the great fish for three days before God rescued him. Jesus Christ was dead and buried Friday night, all day Saturday, and part of Sunday morning before his resurrection on that third day. Whenever John organizes around three, it's a token that God's purposes are at work in some way and the Almighty has determined the outcome.

The number denoting completion or fulfillment is seven. There are seven days in a week, and God rested on the seventh. Seven lamps in the golden lampstand stood in the tabernacle and the temple, denoting God's uninterrupted presence. Priests were consecrated for seven days before entering the priesthood. Blood was sprinkled on the mercy seat seven times to demonstrate complete redemption. Israel marched around the walls of Jericho seven times before blowing their shofars and watching the city fall.

Six is the number of man. Notably, it is a mere digit short of seven, not complete. Human beings were created on the sixth day, just after the birds of the air and beasts of the field. Yes, the serpent was created on that day as well. Man is permitted to work as he wishes for six days, but he must rest on the seventh which belongs to his Creator. A Hebrew slave could only be compelled to serve for six years, after which it was required he be liberated. When Christ attended the wedding at Cana (John 2:1–10,) he saved face for the bridegroom's family by turning water in six stone pots into extraordinary wine. Because the water was used for ceremonial cleansing, the subtext in the Hebrew mind was the efforts of man are always inadequate unless elevated or transformed by the intervention of Christ.

Ten denotes divine authority and obedience. God's covenant gift to his chosen people was the Ten Commandments. Obedience was their token of respect for his authority. The Almighty delivered ten plagues upon Pharaoh and the land of Egypt, a message of authority and a call for repentance. If only ten righteous people could have been found in Sodom, God would have spared the city.

Most of us are aware that twelve is the number of the church. There were twelve tribes in the Old Covenant nation of Israel. Christ called twelve apostles when he laid the foundation of the New Testament Church. Revelation describes the kingdom of heaven as having twelve gates through which the saints of God enter his habitation.

Finally, the number 1,000 is regarded as the number of multitudes. In Deuteronomy 5:10, Moses describes God as someone who punishes sin but shows steadfast love to thousands of those who love him and keep his commandments. Obviously, the literal number must be billions. Or consider Job 9:3, "If one wished to contend with him, one could not answer him once in a thousand times." Even Job didn't try that many times. The number is figurative. According to Psalm 50:10, every creature in the forest belongs to the Lord, as well as "the cattle on a thousand hills." In fact, there are clearly more than 1,000 hills and mountainsides on the earth, and it would seem God owns all of them and their livestock as well. The psalmist used the figure in the customary, metaphorical manner to suggest the incalculable herds of cattle grazing on hillsides around the globe, all on loan from God.

In Revelation, the number 1,000 generally means vast numbers bordering on the incalculable, not unlike God's promise that Abraham's descendants would number like the sand on the beach or the stars in heaven. It rarely means the exact quantity that comes after 999.

## Divine Arithmetic

As you move through the first chapter of Revelation, you will quickly come to a section about seven churches. By the end of the chapter, you'll read about seven stars, in whose midst God is standing. As you'll see, there actually are seven literal congregations John takes the time to mention and later address. But in a world where many churches have been persecuted or even driven into hiding, there are many more than seven who need comfort and encouragement. In selecting seven, God is surely thinking of the complete church, the full church, not merely a handful. Likewise, the stars at the end of the chapter represent seven pastors Christ holds in his hand. Rest assured, there were far more than seven or eight pastors under threat of arrest and prosecution—perhaps dozens or scores at any moment. Again, Christ's promise through the use of the number seven is he is securing all his suffering pastors in his grip.

Jumping well ahead to Revelation 7, we read about 144,000 members of the nation of Israel being sealed. God literally puts the process of judgment on pause until that vast number of the faithful can be placed under his authority and protected. Some read this to mean that at one point just before The End, a revival among the Jews will lead to 144,000 being saved. Precisely 144,000, not one more? And exactly 12,000 from each of the twelve tribes? That may strike you as arbitrary and rather unlikely, but what other choice do we have?

Here's how I believe John's original readers interpreted that figure. We have established twelve is the number of the church. Not surprisingly, one way to show the Old Testament worshippers and the New Testament saints, the entire church multiplying under God's mighty hand would be an equation like $12 \times 12 \times 1,000$, a vast multitude. The product of that calculation would amount to 144,000 being sealed. Of course, knowing what we do about Revelation, we understand that's not a literal number. Rather, it represents vast thousands upon thousands of Old Testament believers and New Testament believers being secured under God's umbrella of protection until Christ returns. It's a hopeful and optimistic count—not a grim limit imposed by an arbitrary God restricting how many can be saved and not a soul more. It's not presented as a warning, like the door to Noah's ark being slammed when the last pair of zebras rush in. In this context, it's more of a glad expectation of something wonderful happening everywhere. How can we suppose that? Because only one brief verse later, in Revelation 7:9, that number of the washed is suddenly too large to count!

By the way, sealing is a powerful term in the gospel. In Ephesians 1:13–14, Paul promises you and me, "In him you also, when you heard the word of truth, the gospel of your salvation, and believed in him, were sealed with the promised Holy Spirit, who is the guarantee of our inheritance." When we come to Christ, we are mysteriously sealed with the Holy Spirit in such a way as to guarantee we will never fall away and will ultimately receive the inheritance promised to us. That's why all those believers in John's vision were sealed. The fact they were all assigned to a tribe is a reassuring reflection of Paul's observation that some of the branches of God's original olive tree were broken off, but a few stray branches of wild olive trees were grafted in (Rom. 11:16–18). There are no Israelites-in-name-only counted among the numberless multitude in Revelation. They are all one people, Jew and Gentile alike, considered by God to be true Jews.

We have more numbers to explore, but we have still more questions to raise and more chapters to conclude. For now, let's pause and give thanks that we belong to the true vine, the uncounted multitude of faith.

## Think about It

1. Revelation 21–22 are chock-full of familiar numbers. Read both chapters and explain what each number in the narrative describes.
2. Look again at 21:4. Realizing every tear will be wiped away by God and that death will be no more, what are "the former things" that have passed away?
3. At the heart of Revelation, we find three cycles of events: seals, trumpets, and bowls. Each contains seven events or periods of time. For the moment just think about what the numbers suggest about those events.

# CHAPTER FOUR

# THE BEAST, THE PROPHET, AND THE MARK OF THE BEAST

*And they worshiped the dragon, for he had given his authority*
*to the beast, and they worshiped the beast, saying,*
*"Who is like the beast, and who can fight against it?"*
—Revelation 13:4

John's Revelation was written around AD 90. If the beast in that vision represented only some cruel tyrant whose power play was well over 2,000 years away, it would have meant absolutely nothing to John's original readers. What could they possibly do about an event so many lifetimes away in their distant future? Jesus emphasized, "Therefore do not worry about tomorrow, for tomorrow will worry about itself" (Matt. 6:34). Since the Lord stated plainly we cannot add a single cubit to our stature by worrying about our height, is it plausible he would have warned first-century saints living on the edge of survival that they should agonize over a fate lurking more than twenty centuries away?

As he chronicled his vision, John was rotting away on a prison isle known as Patmos, and his original readers continued to endure their own great tribulation. They were already familiar with a brute who demanded the entire Roman world worship him, a regime controlling a vast region and using imperial power to wage war on the saints solely because of their offensive faith. Even with the weapons technology of the future at his disposal, could a dictator yet to come inflict any penalty more agonizing and horrendous than crucifixion, facing hungry lions in the arena, or being burned at the stake in the name of Emperor Domitian? In John's case, he was sent away into exile only after he miraculously survived being boiled in oil. Can you imagine a greater tribulation than living every day with the knowledge that brutal forms of death like these may well await you, your family members, and your friends?

We established in chapter 2 the Beast is first described in Scripture by the prophet Daniel. According to Daniel 7:23, the Beast is a "kingdom on earth" different from other kingdoms. This means the notorious figure is a government rather than one powerful or charismatic individual. Our original source defines the Beast not one evil personality, but an entire regime. First, let that sink in. Then, let's take a look at what else we're told about this monster.

**Rev. 13:**—The creature rises from the sea, featuring seven heads, ten horns with crowns, and blasphemous names on his head. The numbers relate to his demand for complete power and the kind of total obedience due to God. Daniel explained the horns and crowns suggest kings who have risen and fallen as a part of this all-powerful regime. Since the sea generally represents human populations in the Old Testament, this government initially boasts of being of the people.

**13:2**—Parts of the Beast resemble a leopard, a bear, and a lion. His power and authority come from the Dragon. As we saw earlier, one of Daniel's visions characterized the Greek Empire as a leopard, the Medo-Persian Empire as a bear, and Babylon as a lion. This kingdom shares qualities with all those plus Daniel's fourth kingdom, which was Rome. This image is a hybrid of all those. In other words, beasts like this come and go. We have seen them before and, tragically, we will encounter them again. We know from Revelation 12:9 the Dragon represents Satan. Governments of this kind generally give public assurances they are there for the common man or woman, but in fact, they are employed by Satan, supported by the powers of hell.

**13:3–4**—The Beast appears to have overcome a deadly wound, so the world rejoices, fawning over the regime, and in their worship of human political clout, they also surrender to Dragon. What do we learn here? Authoritarians like this always create a narrative that they have turned some cosmic emergency or national crisis into a great opportunity. ("Never let a crisis go to waste.") The multitudes who believe the hype are gradually seduced to regard the Beast as being divine and beneficial—the more power, the more benefits. Of course, in bowing at the altar of humanism, they have forfeited human liberty, rejected God, and aligned themselves with Satan.

In other words, the Beast is government trying to be God. The figure represents ruthless governing bodies who virtue signal about rescuing the environment, saving the nation, or leveling the playing field while recklessly pursuing only one goal: absolute control. Inevitably, they seize emergency powers in the name of a shortage resulting from their own bungling or a faux crisis of their own making. Eventually, the emergency ends but the new controls remain firmly in place.

In 1933, while Adolph Hitler and the National Socialists were still fighting for supremacy in Germany, the legislative building known as the Reichstag was mysteriously burned. Denouncing the arson as the work of communists, the Nazis lobbied for emergency powers to hunt down the culprits and end the unrest. Once that law was enacted, the regime leveraged it to eliminate their enemies and strip away other civil rights as well. Of course, many historians believe Nazi sympathizers set the fire in the first place.

**13:5–8**—The Beast will blaspheme against God and make war on the saints, ultimately seducing everyone into total allegiance and worship. His authority will last only forty-two months, or three and a half years. What can we learn from this?

First, hyper-authoritarians always target the church. Believers are the natural enemy of totalitarians because people of the Book always champion human freedom, limits on government, and equal treatment under the law. Those are the first values beastly regimes need to eliminate. What's more, local churches give Christians a natural venue to speak freely, share convictions, and organize in opposition against the Beast. Some totalitarians like the Roman Empire or any number of communist regimes have outlawed the church outright before waging war. Others pretend to be more fair-minded by preaching fairness while quietly undermining freedom of speech and the right to assemble. This is rationalized, of course, as preventing home-grown terror or stopping the flow of disinformation.

Finally, what about the forty-two-month limit, which translates to three and a half years? Notice three and a half is exactly half of seven. Since seven denotes completeness or fulfillment, half is a token of being incomplete or temporary. Because they rise and rule in defiance of the Creator, regimes aspiring to divine authority will eventually crash and burn. The Roman Empire unraveled over three centuries. The brutal Communist regime called the Soviet Union lasted just about seventy years. You can defy gravity for a while, but not forever.

## The Prophet

> It exercises all the authority of the first beast
> in its presence and makes the earth and its in-
> habitants worship the first beast, whose mortal
> wound was healed. It performs great signs, even
> making fire come down from heaven to earth in
> front of people. (Rev. 13:12)

Collective illusion is what happens when individuals go along with an idea they personally oppose, persuaded that most people accept that idea. In other words, the fear of looking foolish is so deeply rooted in most of us that we will accept a lie if we are convinced the majority of our countrymen regard that idea as respectable. That's the basic idea behind the fable of the Emperor's New Clothes. When most of a king's subjects seem to believe the king has paid a fortune for the world's most lavish clothing, the monarch can walk around in public unclothed and unaware of it—until an unsophisticated child laughs, and calls out, "Hey, you're naked!"

Long before the condition had a name, tyrants and their lackeys realized they needed one additional tool beyond money, threats, and armed troops. Social control is managed by "useful idiots," prominent citizens who will parrot the party line and lead trusting neighbors astray in the interest of self-preservation or celebrity. Quite often, a religious movement or sect within a nation will cozy up to the regime to gain an advantage over rival groups. It's groups like that who are described as the second beast, the one from the earth. To avoid confusion, I prefer to identify this beast as the "prophet."

**13:11–14**—This creature has horns like a lamb but speaks like a dragon. It uses its authority to align people behind the Beast, seemingly performing miraculous signs to lead the population to worship the Beast. In the Old Testament, the lamb is an animal of spiritual significance, offered and eaten at Passover. Likewise, the Dragon has a spiritual connotation as the face of evil in the world. The "prophet" counterfeits a likeness to faith while actually advancing the purposes of hell. Hence, God's warning is the Beast will be propped up and supported by a segment of the quasi-religious. The ability to do miraculous signs underscores the spiritual or mystical nature of this Beast.

In first-century Rome, the pagan oracles and priests were cheerleaders for the iron-fisted rule of the emperor and his cronies. They enjoyed a symbiotic relationship by affirming Caesar as divine and worthy of worship, in exchange for favor and protection from the empire. In a very similar manner, today's Russian Orthodox Church is closely aligned with the communist rule of Russia, despite the regime's harsh tactics, the needless slaughter of civilians in the war against Ukraine, and the frequent use of polonium-210 in assassinating critics and dissidents on foreign soil. Just before Putin's reelection in 2012, a leading patriarch lauded his administration as "a miracle of God." In return for its loyalty, the church enjoys favored status and financial assistance from the regime.

As the Beast stretches his tentacles throughout American life today, his most ardent supporter is the environmental movement. The Greenies have developed their own religion in which Mother Nature is a goddess who requires sacrifice for the sins of pollution, species extinction, failure to recycle, or creation of $CO_2$. Unlike other proselytizing religions, environmentalists require draconian legal mandates to force their theology on the unconverted masses. As a result, economies around the world are faltering and farmers must mount massive demonstrations to oppose a radical agenda that squanders fortunes, threatens the food supply, and harms the poor. Green religion has become the prophet for a very hungry Beast.

## The Mark of the Beast

> This calls for wisdom: let the one who has understanding calculate the number of the beast, for it is the number of a man, and his number is 666. (Rev. 13:18)

**13:16–17**—It requires all citizens great and small must receive a mark on the right hand or the forehead, the mark of the Beast. Without this, no one can conduct business or buy and sell. Later in Revelation 14:9–11, we learn anyone who submits to the mark has confessed his allegiance to the Beast and will face the wrath of God and divine judgment.

Is the mark of the Beast some kind of digital computer chip implanted in the body? It's fascinating that an idea from AD 90 could match up so intricately with the economics and technology of the twenty-first century. There's also irony in the fact the Bible anticipates the eventual rise of a one-world government, an idea that looks particularly ominous in the post-COVID age. Of course, these are not nearly the only examples of Scripture being far ahead of its time in describing realities that remained unfamiliar to science for centuries.

I would never assume any feat is impossible for the mind of God. So I can confidently venture the Author of Life can easily establish a spiritual principle and then overlay it with a brilliant prophecy of a scientific advance in the distant future. Nevertheless, the main thrust of

Revelation is spiritual instruction. Detailed scientific forecasting would simply be a by-product of John's Revelation. So let's dig deeper for the timeless truth.

In Ezekiel 9:3–8, the prophet sees a vision of a man dressed in linen, carrying a writing case. He goes through the streets of Jerusalem placing a mark on the heads of men and women who are grieved and offended by the ungodly practices so common in the city. Then God orders anyone not bearing the mark on the forehead must be struck down. This is a sign the people of faith are now in the minority and God has forsaken the city. The next vision will reveal the glory of God leaving the temple.

The principle of holiness, the concept that true faith sets a life apart as distinctly as a mark on the forehead or hand, is an old one in Scripture. It's behind the Passover ritual requiring the blood of lambs be painted on gateposts and doorways to protect the Israelites from the coming judgment (Exod. 12:7). It explains the divine instruction that the words of God should be bound to the hands and foreheads of his people (Deut. 6:7–9). We've already noted that was a figurative expression designed to promote living out the Word of God rather than simply reading it. In the New Testament, the same idea is found in 2 Corinthians 5:17. Paul writes, "Therefore, if anyone is in Christ, he is a new creation. The old has passed away; behold, the new has come." The transformative change that follows faith is always evident.

In John's vision at Patmos, pagans and unbelievers live out a secular ethos that could not be more evident if they were wearing warpaint. They have unashamedly rejected the ancient ways of God to adopt the narrative and fashions of the age. In following the Beast, they have assumed his priorities and his purposes, signing off on his hellish agenda. As a result, their gaze, their interests, and their deeds clearly reflect a godless, secular ethos.

Followers of Jesus cannot bear that mark because our lives are already set apart by a very different set of ideas, the Truth. Today, like never before, your life is an online open book. Advertisers and political campaigns can analyze your data and accurately detect your interests, your passions, your health conditions, your romantic inclinations, and your political affiliations. For anyone watching you for more than a few minutes, your life and expressions demonstrate those allegiances as well.

The mark of the Beast comprises a lifestyle that expresses, *The only things that matter to me are material, I'm here for the party, and I have no interest in the things of eternity.* Whenever a government takes absolute control of a nation, this outlook always makes for easy sledding. People without deep, spiritual convictions are not a threat to ambitious totalitarians. But those irritating Christians . . . that's a different story!

**13:18**—This calls for wisdom: let the one who has understanding calculate the number of the beast, for it is the number of a man, and his number is 666.

Many have tried to use complex calculations based on numerology and the Hebrew alphabet to discover the identity of the Beast. It's quite surprising how many famous names are spelled with letters that total 666 when converted to Hebrew. Nevertheless, the answer here requires wisdom, not complex calculations.

In chapter 2, we established six as the number of man. It is one digit short of seven, the number of completion. In other words, man is born incomplete, unfinished, and unable to fulfill his life mission on his own. That's what six means. And three is the number of God, suggesting God and his purposes are somehow implied whenever things cluster in threes. Now, let's apply a tiny bit of wisdom.

If six is the number of a man failing to achieve his destiny, what do three sixes suggest? Very simply, it represents insufficient men (and women, of course) trying to

be God. They'll never succeed but will wreak a wide path
of destruction in trying, particularly in league with religious movements championed by idealogues with delusions of greatness. In a kingdom in which the authorities
in charge are determined to play God, the mark of the
Beast identifies the comfortably numb multitudes who
have drunk the Kool-Aid or swallowed the blue pill,
utterly seduced by partisans with delusions of divinity.
This integer, 666, is the number of irreligious and unfinished human beings estranged from their Creator, carried away by promises of a  political utopia.

## Think about It

1. With the advent of satellite communication, 24/7
   TV, the internet, smartphones, and social media, do
   you believe collective illusion has become less likely or
   more likely? Why?
2. President Gerald Ford wrote, "A government big
   enough to give you everything you want is a government big enough to take away everything you have."
   How is that true?
3. If we should identify a beast in some random nation
   in the Middle East, which movement or ideology
   might be the most likely candidate for the role of the
   "prophet"? Why?

   - The United Nations
   - The U.S. Embassy, the CIA, and other agents of
     the United States located in that nation
   - Mullahs from one sect of Islam or another

4. Name two or three of your spiritual convictions that
   would make your life incompatible with the mark of
   the beast.

# CHAPTER FIVE

# THE THRONE ROOM OF GOD

*At once I was in the Spirit, and behold,*
*a throne stood in heaven, with one seated on the throne.*
—Revelation 4:2

Many of John's original readers in Rome may have been secretly meeting together in the damp shadows of the catacombs when John's final communique was read to them. Those bleak underground tunnels were the places where saints buried their dead rather than have their bodies incinerated according to Roman custom. Now under penalty of death, some worshipped there as well. We seldom consider that many of the people to whom John was writing were hearing his message in one of the eeriest, most unsettling settings you can imagine. They might as well have been walking through a graveyard after dark.

Do you think anybody complained about John trying to frighten them with these dark, ominous images? Can you imagine parents covering their children's ears or sending them out because this kind of literature was inappropriate? Of course not. They were meeting underground surrounded by crypts and corpses because authentic terror and literal danger threatened above ground every day. John's description of his vision from God was good news, not bad news. What the old apostle had to say gave his readers and listeners confidence, hope, and enough courage to continue living out the gospel and defying the Roman Beast.

Ironically, many mature Christians in the twenty-first century think of Revelation as grim, frightening, or discouraging. In fact, the final book of the Bible is necessarily filled with light, hope, assurances of God's presence, and promises of a final victory that makes it all worthwhile. The first time I spent twelve weeks teaching Revelation to a churchwide Bible study, the congregation spontaneously leaped to their feet in a rousing standing ovation on the final night. I have a feeling those underground saints from the first century had a similar response when they first heard this powerful, motivating message.

As Revelation 4 opens, John has just devoted two chapters to the challenges facing the churches. Corrupted congregations are feeling okay about things, but faithful believers are facing opposition, persecution, and even death. It's an unhappy situation, but it's not breaking news to anyone. The churches who respect John are all too familiar with the injustice. The message resonating with them is God has not lost control or gone into exile. The heavens have not been turned upside down. The God who raised their Savior from the dead is still in charge and keeping promises. The Lord has given his old friend a briefing.

**4:2–6**—After seeing Jesus Christ standing among his afflicted churches on the earth, John lifts his eyes to heaven. There he sees the Ancient of Days seated on the throne, obviously in perfect control. There's an aura about him, like the glow of brilliant light reflected by precious stones in all the colors of the rainbow. Orderly worship continues all around the throne. A sea of glass beneath not only reflects the majestic lightshow happening all about but also means God can see in all directions. Not unlike Mount Sinai, the ongoing, never-ending authority of the Creator is reflected by lightning, thunder, and voices, no doubt the prayers of the saints rising to the throne. Seven lamps of fire represent the Holy Spirit, the totality of God's spiritual power always available to the church.

**4:4**—The identity of the twenty-four elders around the throne is no mystery to those of us who understand Hebrew numbers and biblical history. John recognizes saints from both halves of the story of redemption: the Old Covenant and the New. It's no longer Jew versus Gentile in the church of Jesus Christ. We are all members of the body, adopted sons and daughters of the promise. Twelve tribes of Israel plus twelve apostles equals twenty-four elders bowing at the foot of the throne.

Neither do we have to speculate what the four strange creatures around the throne represent in Revelation 4:6–7. They are covered in eyes, and have the likeness of a lion, a calf, a man, and an eagle. And each one flies with six wings, declaring the holiness of God. We've already established the key to this text is found in Ezekiel 1:1–14. The same four creatures make an appearance there, surrounded by lightning, thunder, and radiance like that of precious gemstones. Ezekiel 1:28 summarizes, "Such was the appearance of the likeness of the glory of the Lord."

Here's the message: Let not your heart be troubled. God is with you, and the wheels of eternity are turning smoothly according to plan in the divine engine room. God is firmly in charge. The loved ones in him you've lost for now are worshipping the Almighty in heaven, the spirit of God is still moving out, and the glory of God is ever-present and undiminished. Don't be deceived by the collective illusion that evil has triumphed once and for all.

## The Highly Classified Scroll

> Then I saw in the right hand of him who was seated on the throne a scroll written within and on the back, sealed with seven seals. And I saw a mighty angel proclaiming with a loud voice, "Who is worthy to open the scroll and break its seals?" (Rev. 5:1–2)

There's no need to use your imagination or consult Bible commentaries to solve the mystery of the scroll with official seals. The answer is found in Daniel 12:4. Around 600 BC, God unveiled the future in a vision for his faithful prophet in Babylon. Just after the Medes and Persians have conquered Babylon and installed a new sovereign, we find Daniel fasting and praying, pleading with God to restore the people of God. An angel, Gabriel, is dispatched to comfort him and unveil a long-term vision of the heavenly rescue plan. Daniel records the details in a long scroll.

That's when God gives the prophet some context and a command. The context for this particular vision written on the scroll is found in Daniel 10:14. "[For I have come] to make you understand what is to happen to your people in the latter days. For the vision is for days yet to come." In other words, unlike his earlier visions which forecast events closer at hand, this long-range vision stretches all the way to the last days, the age beginning with the earthly ministry of the Messiah (Heb. 1:2). The accompanying command is found in Daniel 12:4. "But you, Daniel, shut up the words and seal the book, until the time of the end. Many shall run to and fro, and knowledge shall increase."

Hence, this particular vision of Daniel is related to a future so distant that God commands Daniel should roll up the scroll and seal it until the fullness of time. Images like this reveal something about God, but it's not a suggestion that he still uses scrolls. Rather, Daniel's scroll reminds us God doesn't make impulse decisions on the fly. His purposes are sure, and his plans are so essential that the blueprints have been around since the beginning. Like passengers on a cruise ship, we have free will in making day-to-day decisions, but the captain has his destination programmed into navigation and our world is not in advancing in that sure direction.

The scroll we find in the throne room of God is like the one Daniel sealed. It's been waiting for millennia, maybe longer, to be implemented. Held securely in the hand of God, it waits only for the one authorized to receive it and set the wheels in motion.

## The Lamb

> And between the throne and the four living creatures and among the elders I saw a Lamb standing, as though it had been slain, with seven horns and with seven eyes, which are the seven spirits of God sent out into all the earth. (Rev. 5:6)

In Revelation 5:2–6, almost immediately a question arises. Clearance for this scroll is so elevated only one person is qualified to receive and open it. The sovereign seated on the throne looks long and hard for someone to whom the scroll can be entrusted. But before anyone can panic, the named individual steps up and takes the scroll from the King's hand. Suddenly, all the attention turns to this new figure whom one angel calls the Lion of the tribe of Judah and the Root of David. One verse later, he is described as a Lamb who was slain. He is obviously alive again and is marked with seven horns, seven eyes, and the seven spirits of God.

In the Old Testament, the lamb was the sacrificial animal associated with Passover. Exodus 12:1–7 prescribes each family to select a lamb, a one-year-old male without any scars or blemishes, to be killed at twilight. In addition to eating the roasted meat together, the family will smear or sprinkle some of the blood on the doorposts of their houses as a token for the angel of death to pass over that home. Passover is the Old Testament basis for the Lord's Supper in the New Testament. It anticipates the work of the Messiah.

This Lamb in Revelation is none other than Jesus Christ, the Son of God. He is the Lion of Judah and the Root of David. But there's even more here. He is invested with seven horns, seven eyes, and the seven spirits of God. He stands alongside the throne. The statement with all the sevens indicates Jesus has complete power, sees everything, and has the boundless spirit of God aligned with him. Add the fact he's accepting a document from the Ancient of Days, and he is the only person in the kingdom authorized to unroll this vision of the world's fate and the destiny of the people of God. He alone has the authority to set in motion the next phase of the heavenly plan. Did you notice the eternal transfer of power taking place here?

## Life on a Grand Scale

"I have said these things to you, that in me you may have peace. In the world you will have tribulation. But take heart; I have overcome the world." (John 16:33)

When John wrote Revelation, nearly six decades had passed since the cross, the resurrection, and the ascension of the Lord. Unlike the apostles, most of the followers of Christ in AD 90 never met Jesus of Nazareth or even heard him speak. They were second-generation believers who must have had very little exposure to the Gospels and epistles of the New Testament written so recently. When violent persecution suddenly exploded all around them, we can only imagine how rattled and perplexed they were. This faith was certainly worth living for, but was it worth losing everything?

John's vision reassures them nothing has changed. While Christ was still walking with the Twelve and teaching the multitudes, he explained how following him would not be a walk in the park. "Beware of men, for they will deliver you over to courts and flog you in their synagogues, and you will be dragged before governors and kings for my sake, to bear witness before them and the Gentiles" (Matt. 10:18).

Christ overcame more than death through the resurrection. That alone was earthshaking and world-changing, but it was only part of his work. He first overcame the resistance of the Jewish leaders steeped in centuries of tradition. He overcame the brutal power of the Roman legions who were literally unable to suppress him or crush the fledgling movement he ignited. And he overcame the decadent philosophies of the age and the seductive mythology of Greece and Rome, which captured the hearts of so many. He was already a victor in the clash of cultures when he embraced the cross, drank the cup of death, and blasted away the door of the tomb to emerge alive. And he called us to follow his example as overcomers.

"Truly, truly, I say to you whoever hears my word and believes him who sent me has eternal life. He does not come into judgment, but has passed from death to life" (John 5:24). What does that mean, the idea that a believer has already passed from death to life? John used that same phrase in his first epistle: "We know that we have passed out of death into life, because we love the brothers" (1 John 3:14).

It means when we become followers of Jesus, we stop clinging to the rags of our own existence and hold firmly to the robe of his life. It means we surrender to the truths and traditions of his kingdom even while we remain subject to the laws and customs of terrestrial life. We overcome scorn, resistance, and violent opposition to the reign of Christ because we are in this for his sake, not our own. Fervent love for each other confirms what has occurred.

Our satisfaction and the resulting peace of mind do not come from the absence of stress or the comforts of the upper middle class. Sometimes the consequences of faith are painful. In a world of sin, doing the right thing is never easy, and is seldom rewarded. No, our satisfaction and our confidence must come from him, from being united with him in his death and resurrection.

Holiness on the part of the saints is never easy. But it's essential. And our efforts here are supported by the Lamb of God who still reigns, ever maintaining control of that highly classified scroll in heaven.

## Think about It

1. Read Revelation 4–5 in its entirety. Pause at each figurative phrase or image to remind yourself what it represents.
2. Look again at the four creatures (4:6): the lion, the ox, the man, and the eagle. Knowing the roots of this

image trace back to Ezekiel, what does God obviously have in mind here?

- Matthew, Mark, Luke, and John
- All of creation reflecting the glory of the Creator God
- Russia, China, Israel, and the United States

3. Read 5:9–12 once again. What does it mean that Christ has ransomed people from every age, nation, and language group to make them a kingdom of priests who reign on the earth? Unpack that in your own words.

# CHAPTER SIX

# BABYLON THE GREAT HARLOT

*And on her forehead was written a name of mystery:*
*"Babylon the great, mother of prostitutes and*
*of earth's abominations."*
*And I saw the woman, drunk with the blood of the saints,*
*the blood of the martyrs of Jesus.*
—Revelation 17:5–6

Before there was Rome, there was Babylon. Six hundred years before the birth of Jesus, the capital city of the Babylonian Empire was a cosmopolitan showplace whose grand buildings and temples were constructed of brick and often inlaid with enameled tiles and delicate frescoes. Her streets were paved, arranged in a modern grid pattern. Scenic canals wound through a city whose celebrated hanging gardens were regarded as one of the seven wonders of the ancient world. A ziggurat inspired by Babel towered three hundred feet into the sky, leading one ancient scholar to call it "the foundation of heaven and earth." In addition, education in the city was so advanced they would teach the Greeks a thing or two about astronomy.

Some historians complain that Babylon is much more impressive to archaeologists than to the men who wrote the Bible. Nearly every biblical reference to the city is harsh. But ironically, those same historians concede Babylon is still familiar today largely because of her prominence in God's Word.

While Babylon was still in her glory days, Isaiah foretold the way she would be conquered and left in devastation like Sodom and Gomorrah (Isa. 13:19–20.) But the prophet went further, insisting this particular city of renown would never again be inhabited. Amazingly, although most ancient centers located alongside rivers were eventually conquered and rebuilt time and again, with new buildings atop old ruins, Babylon once again stands out. Though nearly 2,500 years have come and gone since her demise, she has remained barren and uninhabited. Notably, Saddam Hussein drew up plans to rebuild the city as a sort of amusement park and living museum of Iraqi greatness. Prophetically, his vision went up in smoke in 1991 during the carpet bombing of the Gulf War.

Why does God treat such a wonderful world capital so harshly? It's a long story that began badly and only gets worse. When human beings began to migrate and relocate after Noah's flood, a hunter and empire builder named Nimrod established a kingdom called Babel on the Plain of Shinar. Things went south when the inhabitants conspired to build a city whose profile and size would set them apart from every other place on earth. What they undertook was the notorious Tower of Babel. Tragically, their ambition stood in defiance of God's original command that mankind should spread out and fill the whole earth. The Creator's strategic response was to level their ziggurat and confuse their language, forcing them to abandon the scheme and continue to migrate (Genesis 11).

Babel, meaning confusion, eventually gave rise to Babylon, a great city that morphed into a pagan empire. Citizens worshipped a variety of gods and goddesses including Marduk, the king of gods who was sometimes called Bel. Because religious traditions characterized their deities as having all the evil vices and cruel inclinations of the humans who served them, it's no surprise Babylonian culture became unusually merciless and perverse. Children were casually sacrificed or abandoned just like the baby gods and goddesses who were routinely murdered by their divine parents in the Babylonian creation stories. The Greek historian Herodotus described sex slavery and human sacrifice as commonplace in the empire, often inflicted upon neighbors and fellow Babylonians. The empire was well-known for the horrendous brutality exercised on the battlefield and against prisoners of war.

All that bad behavior came from a simple inclination: the arrogant conviction that people were wiser than God. In their pride and unbelief, the Babylonians raised a dark empire determined to overthrow the kingdom of light. But like that mythical golden ring from the Tolkien trilogy, the fierce ambitions driving them would ultimately bring disappointment and destruction.

In 586 BC, the Babylonians invaded Judah, leveled Jerusalem, and relocated the exiles to their pagan homeland. During that era known as the Babylonian captivity, many Hebrew captives became so secularized they chose to remain there even after regime change offered them the freedom to return to Judah. Daniel and his devout comrades were among the uncorrupted minority. You can't miss the seductive power of Babylon in the accounts of the Old Testament.

Of course, Babylon had been on the ash heap of history for centuries by the time John was visited by God on the isle of Patmos. Knowing the characters of Revelation are figurative, we can now ask what world power is represented by the flagrant whore in the apostle's vision?

## The Mother of All Iniquities

John leaves no doubt about the identity of the harlot in his vision, at least in the Old Testament. Her name is Babylon, and the vision matches up with Old Testament descriptions. "Babylon was a golden cup in the Lord's hand, making all the earth drunken: the nations drank of her wine; therefore the nations went mad." (Jer. 51:7)

- "For all nations have drunk the wine of the passion of her sexual immorality . . ." (Rev. 18:3).
- "And Babylon, the glory of kingdoms, the splendor and pomp of the Chaldeans, will be like Sodom and Gomorrah when the God overthrew them" (Isa. 13:19).
- "The woman was arrayed in purple and scarlet, and adorned with gold and jewels and pearls, holding in her hand a golden cup full of abominations and the impurities of her sexual immorality. And on her head was written a name of mystery, 'Babylon the great, mother of prostitutes and of the earth's abominations'" (Rev. 17:4).

When John's original readers began to decipher his apocalyptic code, there was no doubt Rome was the great prostitute of their generation. The depraved harlot rode a beast with seven heads, which an angel explains were the seven mountains on which the woman was located (17:9). Rome was famously situated on seven hills.

John writes, "And I saw the woman, drunk with the blood of the saints, the blood of the martyrs of Jesus" (17:6). Babylon didn't survive long enough to cause a single Christian death, but several Roman emperors sent believers to violent deaths in the arena. The truth of the gospel was not compatible with the demands and requirements of Caesar.

Like Babylon, Rome's wealth, splendor, and opportunities guaranteed anybody who wanted to be somebody in the first century would see her as a stepping-stone. Inversely, it also meant Roman immorality and pagan ideals could easily multiply and spread, even to the most distant reaches of the world.

Many Roman emperors openly practiced pedophilia, often having favored boys castrated to keep them soft and pliable. Children were so disposable that unwanted babies could be abandoned at the city dump to be eaten by scavengers or carried off by human traffickers if they didn't die from exposure. The Roman ethos justified slavery by insisting certain classes of people were born to serve as beasts of burden. For centuries, women had such low status that they could not inherit when husbands or relatives died. Like most other ancient cultures, Romans frowned upon any form of charity or assistance to the afflicted as irreligious. If the gods are punishing your neighbor, why would you interfere by cushioning the blow?

Not surprisingly, Christians undermined all these civic virtues. They rescued abandoned children, raising them as their own. When the death toll from an epidemic drove frightened pagans to cast sick relatives into the streets, followers of Christ took them in to care for them. The church perceived women as heirs in Christ, treating them so favorably that pagan women were among the first to recognize the appeal of the faith. The same was true of the enslaved. Not surprisingly, the first hospitals in Rome evolved from humane care centers organized by believers.

## The Grand Seduction

"And the woman that you saw is the great city
that has dominion over the kings of the earth."
(Rev. 17:18)

Babylon, the Great Harlot, always draws her seductive power from one corrupt nation or another, but she is not political. Rather, she represents the infectious spirit of the age, always promising relevance and freedom, yet perpetually hostile to the ideas of God and his church. Scheming autocrats are her champions.

In Nazi-era Germany, for example, the spirit of the age evolved from the work of Charles Darwin. A novel idea called eugenics ("good breeding") took the theory of natural selection to its logical extreme. If random, unguided evolution could slowly but surely refine a species, the purposeful, intelligent manipulation of the human gene pool could undoubtedly lead to more rapid improvements and the rise of a super race. Within that unforgiving framework, it made sense that the genes of "inferior" people and classes of people should be strictly suppressed. The blacklist of unwanted genes soon expanded from invalids, the mentally ill, and homosexuals to include Jewish people and anyone who sympathized with them. At first, those restricted classes were merely segregated in designated ghettos, but extermination camps were the eventual "final solution."

While it's true Adolf Hitler might have become the most familiar advocate of eugenics, it was not a whacky conspiracy theory championed by people on the fringe. This utopian fantasy that genetic engineering could transform human nature was a mainstream ideal that captivated leaders and intellectuals in Europe, then crossed the Atlantic to intrigue smart Americans as unlikely as Theodore Roosevelt, Helen Keller, and Alexander Graham Bell. Margaret Sanger, the founder of Planned Parenthood, was a thought leader behind the movement. She wrote, "Birth control is nothing more or less than the facilitation of the process of weeding out the unfit . . . of preventing the birth of defectives."[1]

Eugenics was just one prevailing fashion in Europe after the turn of the century. "Anything Goes" was more than a catchy tune. It was a driving philosophy. Friedrich Nietzsche was not dancing on anybody's grave when he warned "God is dead," but other intellectuals gladly embraced his infamous verdict. Gone were those backward Victorian ideas about marriage and monogamy. With human ingenuity now in absolute control, the future was bright and full of possibility. Old restraints could finally be cast off and everyone could eat, drink, and be merry—all the way to the Holocaust and World War II.

For readers of Revelation, Babylon describes the spirit of the age, shapeshifting from generation to generation, but always demanding and deceitful. Multitudes rise to follow because she appeals to the flesh and pretends to be "all-natural." She captivates kings and presidents with her potential and her growing popularity. After all, no one wants to miss the next big idea or wind up on the wrong side of history. The spirit of Babylon gets away with murder because it generally takes a generation for her lies and false promises to reap the whirlwind.

The Great Harlot of our generation wields the wealth and influence of the United States in seducing

---

[1] Margaret Sanger, "The Eugenic Value of Birth Control Propaganda," Birth Control Review (October 1921): 5.

unsuspecting nations around the globe. Popular American movies and music glorify sexual debauchery, same-sex attraction, prostitution, the sexualization of children, and sex-change surgery for minors. Billions of foreign aid dollars once promoting free, democratic elections now push sex-change treatments for children, gay civil rights, transvestitism, and the availability of free abortion. Babylon is more powerful than ever, and the whole world drinks from her jeweled goblet of death.

## Think about It

1. Read Revelation 18. How does the global influence of the United States compare to the seductive power of the Great Harlot?
2. Why is it a given that the spirit of the age will always oppose the people of God and the spread of the gospel?
3. Make a list of five or six core ideas or features of the spirit of the age in the United States at present. What is the gospel antidote to each of those deceptions?

# CHAPTER SEVEN

# THE LAST DAYS

*When the Lamb opened the seventh seal,*
*there was silence in heaven for about half an hour.*
— Revelation 8:1

God relies on repetition for instruction. In the opening chapters of Genesis, he gives us two accounts of the creation, back-to-back. The first account emphasizes the order in which he spoke the cosmos into being and his rationale behind the Sabbath. The second account explores man's relationship to creation. The two perspectives give us different insights into the same event.

Likewise, the New Testament provides us with four different narratives about the earthly ministry of the Messiah. Matthew, Mark, and Luke explore events scattered across the land of Israel, while John centers on time spent in Jerusalem. The first three tend to emphasize Christ's human nature, while the fourth is more focused on his divine nature.

That being the case, it shouldn't surprise us to learn Revelation is organized around three displays of God's final plan for planet Earth. At the heart of John's vision

from Patmos are three chronologies, each in seven parts.
Flip through Revelation and you will find this pattern:

- Seven seals are opened one at a time (6:1–8:5).
- Seven trumpets are blown in sequence (8:6–11:19).
- Seven bowls are poured out on the earth, one after
  the other (16:1–21).

The most familiar view of Revelation explains these
as twenty-one cascading events, each one more terri-
ble and more devastating than the one before. Unfortunately, that approach is so mind-boggling and surreal
that most people don't notice a glaring contradiction.
God can only bring ultimate judgment and melt down
planet Earth one time, but that last straw comes quite
early in the chain of events and is repeated twice.

When the seventh seal is opened, it begins with grim
silence for half an hour. A divine incense burner is hurled
to the earth. The incense represents all the prayers for justice from all the saints over all the centuries (8:4). Think
about that. What follows is a cataclysm with thunder,
rumblings, lightning, and an earthquake. God has just
answered all those prayers with judgment on the earth,
which is immediately immolated.

But wait! What's left for the seven trumpets and seven
bowls? When the seventh and final trumpet heralds justice, voices in heaven shout, "The kingdom of the world
has become the kingdom of our Lord and his Christ"
(11:15). Another voice says, "The time [has come] for
the dead to be judged and for rewarding your servants"
(v. 18). A temple in heaven opens, revealing the ark of the
covenant, and a cosmic shakedown ensues. Once again,
there is lightning, rumblings, thunder, an earthquake,
and hail. Those events all signify the end of life on earth
and the transition to eternity. It's precisely what we saw
earlier with the seventh seal. And by the way, when we

mention the last trumpet, think back to Paul's description of the end. "Behold! I tell you a mystery. We shall not all sleep, but we shall all be changed, in a moment, in the twinkling of an eye, at the last trumpet. For the trumpet will sound, and the dead will be raised imperishable, and we shall be changed" (1 Cor. 15:51–52).

The third chronology follows the same pattern. The seventh bowl unleashes forces culminating with lightning, thunder, rumbling, an earthquake, and great hailstones (Rev. 16:18). If the end of the world feels rather familiar, it's because we've already seen it with the final seal and the last trumpet. Revelation is organized around three complementing accounts of God's plan for final justice on earth. What can we learn from each of them?

## The Seals (6:1–8:5)

In the throne room of heaven, we are shown a scroll with seven seals. Only the Lamb of God has the authority to unseal and read this document, the details of God's plan for final justice as the last days of the earth wind down. The number seven denotes completion. It makes sense for the entire plan to be laid out in this mandate wherein the end of the world will be authorized. In chapter 6, we see each seal removed from that document, one after another.

The first four scenes of judgment follow mysterious riders on horses of different colors. Context tells us the white steed denotes military conquest, the red one brings bloodshed, the black horse represents famine, and the pale horse is death. These forces have arisen time and again throughout the history of mankind: military ambitions leading to wars resulting in bitter living conditions and high mortality rates. We've seen these horses before (Zechariah 1:7–10). It's important to realize that while these tragedies are part of God's plan, he doesn't have to impose them personally. In Zechariah's vision, the horsemen are God's messengers who merely observe and report the events unfolding on earth.

The fifth seal reveals persecution against the people of God. The souls of martyrs can be seen huddled under the altar in heaven asking God, "How long?" These represent the saints who have faced death for the kingdom and are now patiently waiting for divine justice as promised. They are presented with white robes and instructed that they will need to wait just a while longer. These are just some of the saints offering up those prayers being hurled back to earth when the seventh seal is removed.

When the sixth seal is peeled back, the temperature rises sharply. The sun goes black, the moon turns to blood, and the stars in heaven are thrown out of order. These images are explained by texts like Isaiah 13, which warns of the approaching fall of Babylon. The language is apocalyptic: heavenly bodies are thrown into chaos anticipating what is to come (13:9–10). The Day of Pentecost, a much happier event unfolding centuries later, is also foretold in the Old Testament with images of the galaxy being rattled. In this case, the prophet Joel sees the baptism of the Holy Spirit approaching with the sun turned to darkness, the moon to blood, and the heavens filled with fire and smoke (Joel 2:28–32).

The use of hyperbole does not mean Old Testament prophets were deranged liars addicted to exaggeration. Rather, apocalyptic language employs images that allow readers and listeners to sense the extraordinary impact of a distant event. We use similar language when we say an exciting occasion was "out of this world," or when we fear the boss is angry and "heads are going to roll" at the office. The fall of Babylon changed the balance of power and the economy for the ancients. The spiritual impact of Pentecost would "turn the world upside down." The end of the world and our transition to eternity will bring change like no one has ever experienced before!

Don't miss what happens next. After chaos intensifies on the earth and just before the final apocalypse is unleashed, there's an interruption in the chain of events. Suddenly, we are introduced to 144,000 saints in white robes, 12,000 from each tribe of Israel. Then just as suddenly, we see an unnumbered multitude in heaven, people from every language and nationality, all dressed in white and worshipping Christ. Curious, huh? We've already talked about Hebrew numerology. We understand 12 x 12 x 1,000 represents the twelve tribes of Israel times the twelve New Testament apostles times a vast multitude. This is the whole church—past, present, and future, but why are we all depicted here just before the big meltdown?

Please, hold that thought for a couple of pages.

With the seventh seal comes the final immolation of the earth. But you'd be wrong to assume this means God no longer values the planet he designed especially for us. God also designed the Old Testament tabernacle, the ark of the covenant, and three majestic temples over the centuries. He allowed them all to be destroyed when something better was prepared.

## The Trumpets (8:6–11:19)

Now the seven angels who had the seven trumpets prepared to blow them. The first angel blew his trumpet, and there followed hail and fire, mixed with blood, and these were thrown upon the earth. And a third of the earth was burned up, and a third of the trees were burned up, and all green grass was burned up. (Rev. 8:6–7)

The seals show us how the human obsession with power and acquisition brings warfare, bloodshed, famine, and death. The trumpets approach final judgment from a different perspective. They demonstrate how our natural world, once a lush paradise called Eden, becomes fouled, corrupted, and toxic. This echoes the constant cry of the Old Testament that our sins will turn the environment against us.

After Cain murders his brother, God warns him, "And now you are cursed from the ground, which has opened its mouth to receive your brother's blood from your hand" (Gen. 4:11). Moses warns the people of Israel that whenever they defy God, "the heavens over your head shall be bronze, and the earth under you shall be iron" (Deut. 28:23). In the Gospels, Jesus rebukes his hometown of Nazareth, reminding them that during Elijah's lifetime, God afflicted corrupt Israel with a famine lasting three and a half years. The water dried up.

That's the backdrop for the seven trumpet blasts of judgment. First, the land is charred and made unprofitable; then the sea is spoiled; next the rivers and streams are made bitter. All these are Old Testament images. It means the natural world that feeds, waters, and sustains us will become more stressed, more abused, and more fouled over the ages. Of course, there may be momentary upticks where human engineering cleans up one river or restores a few fish to the ocean, but the trendline will be down . . . down . . . down.

The fifth trumpet heralds intense spiritual warfare. Terrifying spiritual forces wage war against humankind. Mercifully, people bearing the seal of God will be spared some of that misery. Everyone else will struggle with the unfairness of life, the emptiness of existence, and the pain of having nowhere to turn when life is at its worst.

The sixth trumpet sees conditions escalate further. The bizarre army of horsemen numbering two hundred million (Rev. 9:16) are not an earthly force but may represent waves of demonic assault like the one intended to derail the ministry of Jesus.

Chapter 9 ends with murders, sorceries, sexual immorality, and thefts. Surprisingly, chapter 10 begins abruptly with John eating a little scroll that denotes the Word of God. Then two witnesses appear preaching the gospel while John is told to measure the temple. They are called two olive trees or lampstands before the Lord (11:4).

The identity of the two figures is found in Zechariah 4. The prophet sees two olive trees standing beside the golden lampstand. When he asks their identity, the angel tells him, "These are the two anointed ones who stand by the Lord of the whole earth" (Zech. 4:14). In the Old Testament, only the king and the priesthood were divinely anointed. In the New Testament, every man or woman who trusts Jesus Christ becomes the anointed. John not only understood this but taught it throughout his ministry. In his first epistle, he encouraged fellow believers: "The anointing that you received from him abides in you, and you have no need that anyone should teach you. But as his anointing teaches you about everything, and is true, and is no lie—just as it has taught you, abide in him" (1 John 2:27).

In this scene, God depicts the church, his anointed, preaching the gospel. Quite often, this feels like breathing fire from one's mouth in the face of a hostile world. The immediate outcome can be martyrdom. They are struck down by the forces of the beast, an arrogant and out-of-control government. But, after three and a half days, a short and incomplete period, they are resurrected. Then the voice of God calls out to them, "Come up here." Enemies watch as they ascend to heaven in a cloud. Resurrection and ascension are the destiny of God's faithful people, in the likeness of Christ.

As the seventh plague is unleashed, chaos descends upon the earth, but worship continues to unfold in heaven. The business of eternity is not disturbed by the administration of justice. The final trumpet brings final judgment to the earth. But why the strange interruption? What are we to infer from the martyred church suddenly being called up to heaven in a cloud? You may have a pretty good idea by now but hold that thought.

## The Bowls (16:1–21)

> The fifth angel poured out his bowl on the throne of the beast, and its kingdom was plunged into darkness. People gnawed their tongues in anguish. (Rev. 16:10)

The seven seals depict growing judgment against ungodly humanity by way of warfare, famine, and persecution. The seven trumpets foretell a different aspect of divine justice; the destruction and corruption of the natural world around us. Now, the seven bowls spill out as God unleashes judgment against the beast, a corrupt government demanding the status of a god.

Notice how this narrative looks far more like the ten plagues of Exodus. As God brought the Pharaoh to his knees by leveling the most popular gods and goddesses of Egypt, he afflicted people with boils and sores, rendered the Nile bloody and useless, turned water into blood, and unfurled a suffocating darkness. Not only do those kinds of spectacles play out here, but the fifth bowl specifically targets the Beast—political leaders like Pharaoh who pretend to have divine wisdom and demand that kind of power. The sixth bowl features kings of the earth and demonic spirits battling one another (16:12–14). Of course, the seventh bowl brings the end of the age.

## The Merciful Interruption

Let's consider the mysterious pattern that's been developing in the face of so much judgment. Between the sixth and seventh seals, we see the church from all the ages, robed in white, suddenly appearing in heaven. Between the sixth and seventh trumpets, John shows us two prophets, the anointed, who are martyred and suddenly ascend to heaven. But did you catch the interruption between the sixth and seventh bowls? Look again.

One moment John describes kings of the earth, unclean spirits coming out of the mouths of the Beast and the false prophet as Armageddon builds to a head. Then, without warning, we come to verse 15. "Behold, I am coming like a thief! Blessed is the one who stays awake, keeping his garments on, that he may not go about naked and be seen exposed!" (16:15–16). The statement is such a mismatch for the context that some translations include it in parentheses. The next verse resumes with Armageddon.

Why does Jesus interrupt the approach of the final world war with a promise to return like a thief in the night for those who are prepared and suited up? The answer is obvious: it's a promise that he will arrive to rescue us just before the final collapse. We don't have to personally experience the bitterest dregs of final judgment. We will be evacuated to heaven!

The seals, trumpets, and bowls are three distinct perspectives of the end times, the age that began with Christ and will end with eternity in heaven. Each of the three cycles reflects physical conditions deteriorating over time. Each concludes with the destruction of the earth. But just before that, each interrupts the cycle with either the church being beamed up to heaven or with the promise of Christ to return for us when it's least expected.

This is the event Paul describes in 1 Thessalonians 4 when he speaks of the Lord descending from heaven, the dead in Christ rising first, and then those who are left rising to meet him in the clouds (4:15–17). This is what Jesus has in mind when he promises to return, "coming on the clouds of heaven with power and great glory. And he will send out his angels with a loud trumpet call, and they will gather his elect from the four winds, from one end of heaven to the other" (Matt. 24:30–31). The mysterious interruption in the end times, just before the seventh and final era, describes the rapture of the church.

Wherever the New Testament mentions the return and the rapture, two instructive ideas are always included. For example, in 1 Thessalonians 5:2, 6, Paul elaborates: "For you yourselves are fully aware that the day of the Lord will come like a thief in the night. . . . So then, let us not sleep, as others do, but let us keep awake and be sober." We are constantly reminded no one can know the date of Christ's return until it arrives. But while we cannot know in advance, we are always instructed to watch; to stay awake; to be alert to the signs of the times.

That means no one can assure you Christ is certain to make his return this year or next year or even within the decade. But I can alert you to some signs of the times you should be watching closely. The morning skies are certainly red!

- The convergence of social credit scores and government-backed digital currency ushers in profound new avenues for controlling citizens and demanding compliance.
- The prevalence of social media through laptops and cellphones leaves young people literally im-

mersed in anti-Christian cultural ideas 24/7. It also means for the first time ever, an event happening in the skies over Israel could be witnessed in real time by people all over the world, even those in buildings or locations where TV screens are not available.

- Reports of demonic activity and even exorcisms are multiplying around the world. Accounts of demon possession, demonic influences, and even the public celebration of Satan are arising in every region of the globe. Even secular commentators are describing the crisis in the West as a spiritual problem rather than a political one.

Happily, the second coming of Christ will be the end of that nonsense, but it won't be the end of everything. Rather, the return of the Messiah will inaugurate the age of eternity, with all the people of God from all ages and all the nations of the earth finally together in heaven. No racial barriers. No language barriers. No oppression. Safe at last. Forever at home.

## Think about It

1. There is abundant evidence the seals, trumpets, and bowls are three perspectives of the same seven phases of judgment. Which resonates most powerfully in your mind?

- The Bible often uses repetition: two consecutive descriptions of creation, four separate Gospels about the ministry of Jesus Christ, etc.
- Each series includes the meltdown of the present earth, which can only happen once.
- All three follow a pattern featuring an interruption between the sixth and seventh events. In all three

cases, the break relates to the church transitioning to heaven.

- Three is the number of God, so we are given three viewpoints of what God has ordained will occur.
- The scroll with seven seals contains God's final plan for the earth. Since the number seven indicates it holds the complete plan, there is nothing left for the trumpets and bowls. They can only elaborate upon what has been decreed in the scroll.

2. Optimists might argue the world is not getting worse. There is less poverty around the globe today, and lifespans are increasing in most nations. Electricity, running water, and education are rapidly spreading to the undeveloped world. Do you think the story of the frog in the kettle applies here, or would you offer a different response?

# CHAPTER EIGHT

# THAT'S A GREAT QUESTION

*They cried out with a loud voice, "O Sovereign Lord,*
*holy and true, How long before you will judge and*
*avenge our blood on those who dwell on the earth?"*
—Revelation 6:10

The final book of the Bible is certainly the most provocative. Martin Luther had reservations about it. Gonzo journalist Hunter S. Thompson, no Bible scholar, loved the "purely elegant little starbursts of writing" and the "wild power of the language." Dwight L. Moody insisted, "If God did not want us to understand the book of Revelation, he would not have given it to us at all." It's impossible to predict how you'll react once you make it through the book, but I hope you'll be inspired and encouraged.

You will certainly have questions, though. So let's devote a few pages to the most obvious concepts you might be wondering about.

# What Is the Apocalypse?

> The revelation of Jesus Christ, which God
> gave unto him, to show to his servants the
> things that must soon take place. He made it
> known by sending his angel to his servant John.
> (Revelation 1:1)

The Bible is so thoroughly interwoven into the foundations of the West that we draw on biblical ideas without even realizing it. For example, secular Americans and even atheists frequently warn of one unprecedented catastrophe or another: the climate apocalypse, the nuclear apocalypse, etc. Activists and pessimists love to invoke the A-word! The English word *apocalypse* comes from the Greek term *apokalupsis*, the actual title of the closing book of God's Word, the word we commonly translate as *revelation*. Unbelievably, it's not a Greek synonym for disaster. In fact, if you're a follower of Christ, it's very good news.

Revelation is the "uncovering" of something previously unknown, how Christ will bring final justice to the earth. Rather than one catastrophic event, an apocalypse is an unveiling that sheds new light on the end times or the last days. The A-word is only familiar to Americans today because of the foundational role of the Bible in the life and culture of our nation.

# What Is the Great Tribulation?

> Then one of the elders addressed me, saying,
> "Who are these, clothed in white robes, and
> from where have they come?" I said to him, "Sir,
> you know." And he said to me, "These are the
> ones coming out of the great tribulation. They

have washed their robes and made them white in
the blood of the Lamb." (Rev. 7:13–14)

Our term *tribulation* comes from a Greek word that can
mean affliction, trouble, anguish, burdens, or persecution. The martyrs here (7:13) are the same heroes described in the Hebrews Hall of Fame. "They were stoned,
they were sawn in two, they were killed with the sword.
They went about in skins of sheep and goats, destitute,
afflicted, mistreated—of whom the world was not worthy" (Heb. 11:37–38). It's not peculiar to any age. Jesus
promised his original disciples and all those to come, "In
the world you will have tribulation. But take heart; I have
overcome the world" (John 16:33). This is such a customary experience for the people of God, Paul preached,
"Through many tribulations we must enter the kingdom
of God" (Acts 14:22).

John uses the term five times in Revelation. Four of
those instances refer to the violent oppression of Christians by governments and fanatical leaders of other sects
and religious groups. The enhanced expression "great
tribulation" occurs twice. In Revelation 2:22, it relates to
a local situation—God's response to a sexual cult in Thyatira. In the context of 7:14, it denotes all the hostility
and warfare waged against the people of God throughout history. Even if you are privileged to live in freedom
and toleration today, outlaw saints in places like China,
North Korea, Nigeria, and a host of Muslim nations
endure a very different experience. In John's vision, life
on a planet corrupted by sin is the great tribulation.

## What Is Armageddon?

And I saw the beast and the kings of the earth
with their armies gathered to make war against

> him who was sitting on the horse and against
> his army. . . . And they assembled them at the
> place that in Hebrew is called Armageddon.
> (Rev. 19:19; 16:16)

The culmination of the long, ongoing civil war waged against God by arrogant politicians and godless regimes is called Armageddon. What began with corrupt Jewish leaders and craven Roman emperors raining terror on the church has continued around the globe over the centuries, following the inroads made by missionaries, church planters, and pilgrims. In 1793, the firebrands of the French Revolution were so captivated by the idea of supreme human reason that they demanded the stifling influence of the Christian faith should be eradicated. In their pursuit of true enlightenment, they punished, prosecuted, and guillotined thousands of their fellow citizens. They defiantly imposed a new calendar onto the nation with ten-day weeks and secular festivals and hymns to replace those of the church. Their ideals eventually failed, but the damage was incalculable.

While spiritual warfare is often invisible, waged in the heavenlies, it frequently breaks through in one nation or another as the Dragon raises his latest version of the Beast, and the false prophet begins stirring up the mob. That being the case, it's both biblical and intuitive to assume the intensifying conflict in the spiritual domain will finally spark one final conflict on earth.

As the spiritual civil war comes to a climax, invisible demonic spirits unleashed by the Beast will call up a visible alliance of kings and rulers under one false flag or another. Whatever the stated reason, the real motives will be spiritual ones. With the violent opposition and distrust Israel continues to experience on the world scene today, we can easily conceive how a militarily strategic site near Megiddo could become the focal point of international concerns.

The battlefield mentioned by John, the Plain of Jezreel, has long been a coveted stronghold where pivotal battles have been won or lost throughout history. As recently as World War I, General Allenby led the British to defeat the Turks there. In the sixteenth century BC, Thutmose III defeated an alliance of Canaanites in the same area. Old Testament heroes like Deborah, Barak, and Gideon relished their victories on the Plain of Jezreel. Perhaps most significantly, King Saul was defeated and killed there on Mount Gilboa in a conflict with the Philistines. He died after being rejected by God during his campaign to assassinate David, the Lord's anointed.

With that kind of history, Megiddo provides a striking backdrop for the final struggle of uncontrolled government against the One True God. Like Saul, the delusional kings of the nations will discover they aren't big enough to defy the King of kings.

Two elements of the final war are striking here. First, the rapture happens (16:5) just before the armies assemble at Armageddon. This denotes the church will be beamed up to heaven for a marriage supper before the first explosions of the doomed world. Second, Revelation 19:11, describes Christ appearing in glory, riding a white steed, leading the armies of heaven to crush the rebellion once and for all. Here, Revelation sets the stage for a literal divine entrance never to be forgotten. (For details of Christ's return, see the next question.)

Not long after the church vacates the planet, the corrupt governments of the world will detect a serious security threat underway in Israel. Of course, this will be far more than a military incursion against Palestine or some other nation in the Middle East. Perhaps the United States will still be allied with Israel, requiring a counterstrike against Russia or China. Whatever follows will be the beginning of the end, Armageddon.

## Is the Return of Christ Literal?

> Then I saw heaven opened, and behold, a white horse! The one sitting on it is called Faithful and True, and in righteousness he judges and makes war. His eyes are like a flame of fire, and on his head are many diadems, and he has a name written that no one knows but himself. He is clothed in a robe dipped in blood . . . (Rev. 19:11–13)

Revelation depicts God's plan and the return of Christ to the earth in figurative images, riding a stallion, a sword in his mouth and crowns stacked on his head. While that's instructive, this climax of human history is also described in literal terms throughout the New Testament. Most notably, in all four Gospels, Christ promises to physically return for his church. He describes coming visibly amid the clouds in Matthew 24:30 and Mark 14:62. Luke 12:40 records the warning that his return will occur suddenly, "at an hour you do not expect." And in John 21:22, the Lord responds to a question about John's future by asking, "If it is my will that he remain until I come, what is that to you?" After Christ's ascension in Acts 1:9, angels promise the wonderstruck onlookers, "This Jesus, who was taken up from you into heaven, will come in the same way as you saw him go into heaven."

What will that look like for saints still waiting on earth? "Just as it was in the days of Noah, so will it be in the days of the Son of Man. They were eating and drinking and marrying and being given in marriage, until the day when Noah entered the ark, and the flood came and destroyed them all" (Luke 17:26–27). It was Christ who compared his return to the days of the flood. You may recall the rain did not begin until the day Noah and his family were secured in the ark (Gen. 7:11–13). Still, they were safely out of sight when the torrents began to descend from the heavens and rush forth from the ground below.

In the same way, the day of the Lord's return will seem just like so many other workdays or weekends before—until it's not. People will be shopping, celebrating marriages, and watching sports events. Governments around the world will be angrily muttering about the latest outrage in Israel, but that's been the rule for generations. A deafening shout will rattle the heavens and resonate throughout the cities and countryside of the fateful planet. One long, final trumpet blast will herald the imminent arrival of the King of kings. That's how Paul forecasts the scene (1 Thess. 4:13–18). We can imagine clouds in the sky beginning to churn around the globe. Over Israel, the armies of heaven will appear, robed in blazing white, and preceded by the conquering King, returning to quash the ongoing civil war once and for all.

The dead will rise first, perhaps visibly or maybe so instantly that the human eye can't detect it. It's when the saints still on earth will ascend into heaven, either visibly or in a nanosecond faster than the blink of an eye. This triggers the next and final phase of God's plan.

## What Is the Millennium?

Then I saw thrones, and seated on them were those to whom the authority to judge was committed. Also I saw the souls of those who had been beheaded for the testimony of Jesus and for the word of God, and those who had not worshiped the beast or its image and had not re-

> ceived its mark on their foreheads or their hands.
> They came to life and reigned with Christ for a
> thousand years. (Rev. 20:4)

The *millennium* is the term adopted by the church to
describe the rule of Christ mentioned in Revelation 20.
John employs the figure "one thousand years," but we
have already acknowledged the images in Revelation are
figurative, and the numbers have meaning according to
Old Covenant numerology. The Hebrew connotation for
one thousand points to a vast number that can scarcely be
counted. Earlier we alluded to Psalm 50:10, which assures
us God owns the cattle on a thousand hills. He owns them
all, but that particular number implies an infinite scale.

Although some people insist this is a futuristic political reign that takes place after the meltdown, when God
sets up a new earth, the Bible emphatically teaches Christ
is reigning now. One of my favorite texts is the Great
Commission, familiar to many: "Go therefore and make
disciples of all nations, baptizing them in the name of
the Father and of the Son and the Holy Spirit, teaching
them to observe all that I have commanded you. And
behold, I am with you always, to the end of the age"
(Matt. 28:19–20). We commonly overlook the basis for
that command, found in the previous verse. "And Jesus
came and said to them, 'All authority in heaven and on
earth has been given to me'" (v. 18).

Shortly after the resurrection, when Jesus gave march-
ing orders to his church, he had already been granted
all authority in heaven and on earth. What's left to give
after that? Nothing. Christ was already reigning when he
ascended to heaven.

Other texts assert the idea that Christ reigns today:

- "I saw in the night visions, and behold, with the
  clouds of heaven there came one like a son of man,

and he came to the Ancient of Days and was presented before him. And to him was given dominion and
glory and a kingdom, that all peoples, nations, and
languages should serve him . . ." (Dan. 7:13–14).

- ○ The context here is the fourth beast, the Roman
  Empire, is being defeated on the earth, and the
  scrolls are being unsealed as in Revelation 5.
- ○ At that time, Christ approaches the Ancient of
  Days who transfers authority over to him.
- "Then comes the end, when he delivers the king-
  dom to God the Father after destroying every rule
  and every authority and power. For he must reign
  until he has put all his enemies under his feet" (1
  Cor. 15:24–25).
  - ○ "The end" is about Christ returning authority to
    the Father. In the meantime, the Father has given
    all authority to his Son.
  - ○ Christ's reign continues until he has put all his
    enemies under his feet. That process is underway
    now.
- "You have crowned [Jesus] with glory and hon-
  or, putting everything in subjection under his feet.
  Now in putting everything in subjection to him, he
  left nothing outside his control" (Heb. 2:7–8).
- "The one who conquers I will grant him to sit with
  me on my throne, as I also conquered and sat down
  with my Father on his throne" (Rev. 3:21). He has
  already been seated.

The fact that Christ reigns in the here and now was taught
by the brightest minds and the most respected voices of
the ancient church. Clement of Alexandria, Origen, and
Jerome understood the millennium as a present reality.
Augustine wrote, "During the 'thousand years' when the

devil is bound, the saints also reign for a 'thousand years' and, doubtless, the two periods are identical and mean the span between Christ's first and second coming."

The reign of Christ is such a joyous and liberating idea that it inspired a beloved hymn all of us sing with passion. One of your favorite Christmas carols exults, "Joy to the world, the Lord is come! Let earth receive her King." The third verse assures us, "He rules the world with truth and grace/ And makes the nations prove/ The glories of His righteousness/ And wonders of His love/ And wonders of His love/ And wonders, wonders, of His love." Isaac Watts penned those words in 1719, and they still bring smiles to our faces every year!

## When Will Satan Be Bound?

> And he seized the dragon, that ancient serpent, who is the devil and Satan, and bound him for a thousand years, and threw him into the pit, and shut it and sealed it over him, so that he might not deceive the nations any longer, until the thousand years were ended. After that he must be released for a little while. (Rev. 20:2–3)

During his earthly ministry, Jesus explained to Pharisees and skeptics that he had bound Satan, using that precise terminology. In Matthew 12, envious hypocrites sneered that Jesus could only cast out demons because he was working for Satan. Christ challenged them with pure logic: a house divided against itself cannot stand; neither can a kingdom. Then he added, "Or how can someone enter a strong man's house and plunder his goods, unless he first binds the strong man? Then indeed he may plunder his house" (Matt. 12:29).

That binding could not mean Satan had been destroyed or banished from the cosmos. Rather, it could only mean he had been restrained or limited (i.e., tied up) in some way. That may explain the sudden appearance of demons when Jesus began his ministry. It's significant that demons virtually never appear in the Old Testament; they become an epidemic when Christ arrives then begin to fade (Acts) and never show up through the New Testament epistles. I've always believed Satan was forced to delegate his work to lesser creatures because the Lord somehow restrained him. At any rate, in Revelation 20, John employs the same Greek word, *deo*, Jesus used to explain his success against demons.

It's worth noting that whatever this binding implies, it will be momentarily lifted just before the physical return of Christ. "And when the thousand years are ended, Satan will be released from his prison and will come out to deceive the nations that are at the four corners of the earth, Gog and Magog, to gather them for battle." Revelation 20:7–8 describes a season just before the end when Satan is once again free to operate so his ultimate defeat and judgment can follow. If things seem more hellish lately, there may be a good reason.

## Is This a Premillennial Approach?

Blessed and holy is the one who shares in the
first resurrection! Over such the second death
has no power, but they will be priests of God
and of Christ, and they will reign with him for a
thousand years. (Rev. 20:6)

The three millennial categories often used to explain Revelation are so unfamiliar and misunderstood that I'm not sure they are descriptive anymore. When people ask about my interpretation, here's what I tell them. Revelation is a figurative description of real events which are already unfolding in our world, and every figure is first explained in the Old Testament. It's not original with me. The most respected leaders of the ancient church—Origen, Augustine, and Jerome—understood John's vision much like I do. This school of thought doesn't explain things away or treat John's vision as a parable. To the contrary, Revelation makes more sense and has a practical impact on everyday life when we take John's method seriously.

Men like Augustine believed the first resurrection was the raising of the soul, described by Paul as being buried with Christ in baptism, then raised to walk in newness of life (Rom. 6:4). Similar texts characterize our faith transformation as making us new creations, allowing us to be seated in the heavenlies with Christ (2 Cor. 5:17; Eph. 2:6). The second resurrection is the raising of the body at the return of Christ. The second death is the final judgment in which unbelievers are forever cast from the presence of God.

## Think about It

1. Read Revelation 20. Take a moment to define what is meant by first resurrection and second death.
2. The Great Tribulation has been underway in every generation since the earthly ministry of Jesus. Take some time to pray for saints facing serious persecution and death around the globe today. For prayer concerns or names, do an online search, or visit the Voice of the Martyrs website.
3. Read the lyrics of "Joy to the World." Think about the full meaning of that original confession of the church, Jesus is LORD!

# CHAPTER NINE

# LESSONS FROM EPHESUS AND SMYRNA

*"But I have this against you, that you have abandoned
the love you had at first. Remember therefore from where you
have fallen; repent, and do the works you did at first.
If not, I will come to you and remove your lampstand
from its place, unless you repent."*
—Revelation 2:4–5

## Love by Faith. Selflessly. Tirelessly. Hopefully.

Speaking for Christ, John levels a serious charge against the believers at Ephesus: they have lost their first love. What can that possibly mean? The most popular explanation offered in books and sermons is the Ephesians have allowed their faith to become a meaningless ritual. After going through the motions of worship, witness, and compassion for years on end, they have lost their passion for Christ and their desire to know him. That sometimes happens in churches today, so it makes great fodder for preaching. But is that the problem in Ephesus?

The letter concedes twice that they are bearing up patiently under persecution "for my name's sake." Is it likely religious people who have lost their passion for Christ would be willing to suffer for him, just for the sake of calling upon his name? Unserious people without spiritual passion would be more likely to fold under fire and wait for safer times in the future.

The key here is John's specificity. "You have abandoned the love you had at first." We know how the believers loved at first because it was their trademark. God designed it as the quality that would set believers apart. It's defined in one of the mountaintop moments of John's Gospel and then repeated throughout his epistles. "A new commandment I give to you, that you love one another: just as I have loved you, you also are to love one another. By this all people will know that you are my disciples, if you have love for one another" (John 13:34–35). The Great Commandment encouraged the saints to love God with everything they had and to love others as they loved themselves, but it was the love for one another that would set them apart.

The believers in Ephesus are still passionate enough about God to stand up under fire and cling to their faith in dangerous times. What's been lost is the tenderness and grace they once demonstrated for one another. We learn they've faced huge adversity dealing with false teachers. They are constantly on guard against charming, well-spoken men and women importing deadly ideas into the church. They must screen new arrivals for wrong ideas about the deity of Christ, the nature of the resurrection, the timing of the Lord's return, and even the correct response to sin. Some have come to Christ while still assuming the sexual immorality of their pagan cities was natural and acceptable. It's easy to understand how, over time, this has led some of the Ephesians to be suspicious, defensive, arrogant, and even proud of their own purity.

Could Christ have written to Ephesus first because their problem would become so common among local churches for ages to come? Without a doubt, one of the thorniest problems in church life today is dealing with devoted church members who suddenly become bitter and unloving. Because they've been connected and constructive for many years, it's very easy for their unkind attitudes to attach to others who trust and respect them. What went wrong and what can be done?

At Ephesus, the cynicism resulted from a change in focus. In dealing with so many false teachers infiltrating the church, they gradually shifted their focal point from the love of God to the sins of other people. It must have begun to feel like their security depended entirely on identifying every noxious idea and detecting every last Gnostic or humanist. In fact, their standing was dependent on the power of their loving God; always had been and always would be. They simply got tired and set their affections on things below.

We aren't very effective in screening out dangerous ideas today, but we are very proficient at falling out of step with Christ and linking our behavior to lesser things. Personalities can become too important when a friend disagrees with someone else in the church. Rather than praying and helping our friend keep his spiritual balance, we draw too close and lose ours. Social issues can be divisive when I sense most people at church have a conviction that's different than mine. Instead of focusing on Christ who unites us, I can choose to dwell on the issue and become divisive. Then, of course, there are the sacred cows: practices and programs at church that are so familiar it would make us sad to replace them. We forget the tabernacle and both Jewish temples were all God's idea, but he left them all behind in advancing the gospel.

How do you move on when your emotions get stuck in a bad place? Notice how John counsels his friends at Ephesus. "Remember therefore from where you have fallen; repent, and do the works you did at first" (Rev. 2:8). John warns them to remember, repent, and return.

- Remember what it was like when you walked in unity and refused to be prickly.
- Repent of being overcome by anger and misplaced priorities.
- Return to the ethic of graciously loving other people the way God loves you.

Reconciliation should not be difficult for the people of God. It's the heart of our ministry. Having been reconciled to God, we accept the mission of using our influence and energies to see others reconciled to him as well. It's not simply one option for us among a vast number of mission statements we can choose. In fact, Paul was advocating reconciliation when he wrote, "For the love of Christ controls us, because we have concluded this: that one has died for all, therefore all have died; and he died for all, that those who live might no longer live for themselves but for him who for their sake died and was raised" (2 Cor. 5:14–15).

As a believer, the most compelling force in my life is the love of Christ. No one else has ever afforded me the life-changing benefits he has won on my behalf. No friend, family member, or benefactor has ever loved me as fully and unconditionally as he has loved me. Whenever I recognize friction between his outlook and mine, something must change in me.

Psalm 133 has always been one of my favorites. "Behold, how good and pleasant it is when brothers dwell in unity! It is like the precious oil on the head, running down on the beard, on the beard of Aaron, running down on the collar of his robes!" (vv. 1–2). Read the entire psalm. David describes the way priests were anointed: not merely with a touch of oil on the forehead, but with the sacred oil being poured generously, saturating the garment and filling the air with fragrance.

Neighbors knew instantly when a priest was being anointed because the scent of the precious anointing oil filled the air and drifted in the breeze. That's what the love of God's people for one another accomplishes in our world today. People can't really see our love for God because our habits and disciplines might be rooted in a number of motives. But everyone can recognize when the people of God love each other tirelessly and sacrificially. And Satan wins the advantage whenever we don't.

How can we work on finding the balance between hating sin and loving people?

*Prayer:* Examine your life before the Lord each day, confessing specific sinful attitudes and actions, and thanking God for his gracious forgiveness.

*Discipline:* In conversations, cultivate the habit of listening twice as much as you speak (Eccl. 5:2).

*Attitude:* When you learn someone accountable to you has failed spiritually, pray before responding. First, confirm what happened. Second, being empathetic, offer correction with gentleness and respect (2 Tim. 2:25).

## Choose a Good Death Over a Craven Life

"Do not fear what you are about to suffer. Behold, the devil is about to throw some of you

> into prison, that you may be tested, and for ten
> days you will have tribulation. Be faithful unto
> death, and I will give you the crown of life."
> (Rev. 2:10)

Imagine yourself and your friends worshipping at the
church of Smyrna on Sunday morning. You sing pas-
sionately about Christ being your rock, your identity, the
center of your lives. Some are raising their hands, teary-
eyed. Then the band sits down, and the pastor rises. He
confirms a new hate speech law is now in effect. The
gospel has been forbidden as hateful. Arrests and capital
charges are in the wind. Within weeks, some of you may
well be in prison, on trial for your lives. Others of you
will see loved ones dragged off and many will lose their
property. (For the record, hate speech laws have been
broadened in the United Kingdom and Canada even as
this is being written.)

"But we'll never retreat," the pastor assures you. "We
have a promise from God. 'Be faithful unto death and I
will give you a crown of life.'"

How would you respond? Do you have the same feeling I have—that many U.S. churches would be nearly
empty a week from Sunday? Well, what many twenty-first-century church members will never countenance,
the saints at Smyrna have been enduring for a while as
John writes to them. "I know your tribulation and your
poverty (but you are rich)," he encourages them. "And
the slander of those who say that they are Jews and are
not, but are a synagogue of Satan" (Rev. 2:9). These
godly people rest on the lowest rung of society—much
like the Macedonians a generation earlier—but in the
eyes of God they are overcomers.

The saints at Smyrna have not been seduced by the
shallow comforts of heaven on earth. They are holding
out for a welcome in heaven. John tells them they will

be tested for ten days, meaning God has ordained this temporary measure that will test their obedience. Some of them will suffer. Some of them will die. All of them will overcome. "Be faithful unto death," the Lord speaks truth to them. "And I will give you the crown of life."

Unlike those before us, we have become a mushy generation of uncertain men and women living in denial. Many churches quickly cancel worship services because of light snow, undisturbed that local teenagers are going to work at Dunkin Donuts in the same weather conditions. We are discouraged by the risk of a fender bender or the prospect of worship with a tinier crowd than usual. But earlier generations understood the cost of singing "I have decided to follow Jesus." That price tag could entail persecution, imprisonment, and the loss of their lives. "No turning back. No turning back."

Warriors in the military routinely risk death for the cause of serving our country and defending one another. Police officers and fire rescue teams face death to maintain law and order or save property belonging to others. Extreme athletes risk dying for the adrenalin rush of going higher, farther, or faster. For what priority are we in the church willing to risk difficulty and death?

The bold manner in which early followers of Christ calmly faced death jolted the Roman Empire and shone a light on brutal secular values. A generation after Revelation was written, the public burning of Polycarp, the Bishop of Smyrna, moved pagan onlookers to confess Christ. Centuries later, the determined way Irish priests faced brutality ultimately brought the Vikings to their knees and faith in Christ. We deceive ourselves here in the twenty-first century when we assume our generation rejects our faith because they think we are too extreme. On the contrary, the core reason secular people reject our facsimile of Christianity is they don't believe it makes any difference. We are too easily intimidated by feckless, heartless, childish opponents because we lack courage. Our words and example challenge no one.

Because genuine faith is about change and non-conformity, it always demands risk-taking. Reflect on just a sampling of relevant texts.

- "Be strong and courageous. Do not fear or be in dread of them, for it is the LORD your God who goes with you. He will not leave you or forsake you" (Deut. 31:6).
- "Now when they saw the boldness of Peter and John, and perceived that they were uneducated, common men, they were astonished. And they recognized that they had been with Jesus" (Acts 4:13).
- "The following night the Lord stood by him and said, 'Take courage, for as you have testified to the facts about me in Jerusalem, so you must testify also in Rome'" (Acts 23:11).
- "It is my eager expectation and hope that I will not be at all ashamed, but that with full courage now as always Christ will be honored in my body, whether by life or by death" (Phil. 1:20).

Would I be willing to die for my faith in some future persecution? Honestly, there's no way to know with certainty how anyone will behave in some future event. There's only one advance indicator: the priorities and attitudes driving my life today. How often do I allow my faith in Christ to lead me into the discomfort zone? If I am risk-averse in routine financial and professional matters today, it's likely I'll be the same way with my life tomorrow.

I've found practical encouragement in 1 Peter. "But even if you should suffer for righteousness' sake, you will be blessed. Have no fear of them, nor be troubled, but in your hearts honor Christ the Lord as holy, always being prepared to make a defense to anyone who asks you for a reason for the hope that is in you; yet do it with gentleness and respect" (3:14–15). The aging apostle was eventually crucified upside down. In this text, he not only encourages us to live fearlessly but tells us how to prepare.

Daily devote time to giving thanks to Christ and mentally aligning yourself with his kingdom, his purposes, and his call on your life. Then prepare and rehearse a clear answer you can offer anytime the question arises of why you believe what you say. Once you have that statement of faith, you can gently introduce it in conversations even before someone asks why you see it that way.

*Prayer:* Ask God to give you a fearless heart, and help you replace anxiety and aversion to risk-taking with faith and confidence.

*Discipline:* Be intentional about walking with Christ into the discomfort zone. If your financial giving to the kingdom seems reasonable, notch it up one degree to unreasonable. Begin joining conversations about life and hot topics, offering a faith perspective. If you're unsure of where you should stand on the issue of the day, enter the conversation this way:

- ✓ Mention that you have devoted your life to Christ and want to live with love and integrity, but you are still working through this issue.
- ✓ Then ask rational questions and listen to their answers. For example, if someone insists that human life is no more valuable than animal life, ask them to elaborate. For example, killing roaches and other pests is routine. Why can't we kill pesky people as well?

*Attitude:* Spend time thinking and praying about an attitude of surrender to Christ.

Practice the simple confession, "Here I am, Lord. Send me."

## Think about It

1. Read Revelation 2:1–11. Think about what is meant by the rewards promised: eating from the tree of life and being saved from the second death.
2. Why is it easier to identify and condemn sin in the life of a stranger than to recognize your own spiritual failings and address them? Why it is more constructive to see and deal with yours first?
3. Imagine yourself in the shoes of a hardened, Roman centurion helping with a crucifixion. You have bludgeoned enemies to death on the battlefield. You have nailed dozens of criminals to crosses, standing watch as they died. Nothing can shock you. So what manner of death would bring you to say of one victim, "Surely, this was the Son of God?"

# CHAPTER TEN

# LESSONS FROM PERGAMUM AND THYATIRA

*"But I have a few things against you: you have some there*
*who hold the teaching of Balaam, who taught Balak to put*
*a stumbling block before the sons of Israel so that they might eat*
*food sacrificed to idols and practice sexual immorality.*
*So also, you have some who hold the teaching of the Nicolaitans."*
—Revelation 2:14–15

## Be Holy. Stop Trying to Be Relevant

Pergamum is such a hotbed of pagan worship and idolatry that the Lord calls it Satan's throne. We can only imagine the hostility endured by the church there. Even so, the believers have been bold and tireless, prompting Christ to commend them for their tenacity. "Yet you hold fast my name, and you did not deny my faith . . ." (2:13).

So what's going on with the members who have picked up bad habits from Balaam or the Nicolaitans? Balaam was a mysterious Old Testament mystic hired to stop the Hebrew caravan advancing out of Egypt. He concluded God would not allow his people to be cursed, but maybe they could bring judgment down on themselves. What if they were persuaded to lighten up and live a little, becoming as corrupt as the pagan Moabites they met along the way (Num. 22–25)?

Centuries later, the Nicolaitans rationalized that believers could join their pagan neighbors in immorality because the Holy Spirit was surely strong enough to overcome a few minor indiscretions. This would make the gospel kinder and more compatible with pagan lifestyles.

To some this may sound like nothing more than tolerant, pragmatic faith: Gospel 2.0. To Christ, it sounds like war (Rev. 2:16). And when he calls them to repentance, it's a call transcending time and generations. Worldly software updates have taken root in churches today as well. And it's generally done in the name of being relevant and relatable.

"Making the gospel more welcoming to secular people" always sounds like a fresh, original idea. Meanwhile, a timeless principle taught throughout the Bible is abandoned. How often do you hear church people pray for themselves or anyone else to become more holy?

"Be holy as I am holy." It's found in the Old Testament and the New, but what is it? For a generation, it was defined by the things one didn't do: social conventions, recreation, styles of dress, etc. In fact, the word *holy* is more positive than that. It means I walk a different path because of a divine purpose. What would holiness through purpose look like?

Christ's inaugural message, the Sermon on the Mount, is a great place to start. Here are a few of the aspirations cultivated by the Beatitudes, Matthew 5:1–10:

- Spiritual poverty: I'm not The Greatest. I humble myself in favor of God and others. My greatest asset is the grace God has shown in loving me and forgiving me.
- Mourning: Celebrating life is a good thing, but I must also be empathetic to the broken hearts and shattered lives all around me.
- Gentleness: I discipline myself because I want to be self-controlled, slow to anger, and quick to hear the words of others.
- Hunger and thirst for righteousness: It's not enough to be nice, whatever that means. I want to honor the name of Christ, no matter how demanding that may be.

The challenge for most of us is to stop worrying about what the world thinks of our faith and consider what God thinks about it. Cynics can always find a reason to reject God. They dismissed John the Baptist as a fanatic, and Jesus as a liberal (Matt. 11:18–19). We'll never move unbelievers an inch by being like them. Impact comes when *they recognize* we have different lives because we have a different answer. Beware of those who freshen up the gospel with current fashion or philosophy.

Train yourself in the mindset that time is your most limited resource. Wasted time is wasted life. Paul coached Timothy, "Share in suffering as a good soldier of Christ Jesus. No soldier gets entangled in civilian pursuits, since his aim is to please the one who enlisted him" (2 Tim. 2:3–4). A seasoned warrior can always identify the mission. What's yours?

To the one who overcomes, Christ promises hidden manna and a white stone with a new name. Hidden manna represents the abiding presence of Christ feeding us from within. The white stone alludes to the Roman Olympic games in which the winner was awarded a white stone with his name on it. When we overcome the world, Christ inhabits us, feeds us, and awards us a new name (Rev. 2:17).

How can ordinary people like you and me help bring holiness back to the front burner in our churches? It's a movement that begins one saint at a time.

*Prayer:* Read through Paul's prayer in Ephesians 1. Make note of the specific things he prays the Ephesians will know and experience. Then go back and pray for those specific insights and experiences in your life and the lives of those you love.

*Discipline:* Identify one gift or act of service God has equipped you to make or carry out in the next thirty days. Pray about it. Make it lavish. Carry it out. Keep it private.

*Attitude:* Meditate on the confession, "God, be merciful to me, a sinner!" (Luke 18:13).

## Your Body Is God's Temple. Dedicate it.

> "I know your works, your love and faith and service, and patient endurance, and that your latter works exceed the first. But I have this against you, that you tolerate that woman Jezebel, who calls herself a prophetess and is teaching and seducing my servants to practice sexual immorality and to eat food sacrificed to idols." (Rev. 2:19–20)

How devastating is sexual immorality to the life of faith? Consider the church at Thyatira. They faced suffering and persecution without missing a beat. Christ commends them for their historic acts of love and service, the recent ones even more impressive now than when they first began (Rev. 2:19). Tragically, a prominent woman who advocates sexual immorality has been allowed to build a following in the church. As a result, the assembly is now so infected and the process of uprooting the woman will be so exhausting and painful that Christ concedes he can ask nothing else of them (2:24)!

That should be a wake-up call to followers of Christ in this generation. Half a century after the Sexual Revolution, many young Christians see no conflict between their faith and the debauchery of secular culture. Casual sex, friendship with benefits, shacking up, same-sex relationships, pornography, and gender reassignment are all legit in the minds of youthful multitudes. If the slightest conflict should occur, the church is expected to make concessions.

In the secular quest to redefine human nature, "new" is always good, and God is dismissed as ancient and obsolete. He's wrong about the purpose of sex. "It's fun, and there's nothing sacred about it." He's wrong about homosexuality. "What harm could there be?" He's wrong about marriage. "It's unrealistic and too restrictive." He's wrong about male and female. "Gender is a spectrum, not two complementing designs." And what could possibly be wrong with a man having some fun with online porn? "Only a Puritan could object!" Never mind all these tragic mistakes deny the wisdom and authority of God. All have made their way into the hearts and minds of young people who show up for worship on Sundays.

For centuries, even unbelievers understood the centrality of the sexual ethic within the church. Hedonistic types avoided churches and Bibles like the plague for that very reason. Skeptic philosopher Aldous Huxley wrote about it later in life. "For myself, as no doubt for most of my friends, the philosophy of meaninglessness was essentially an instrument of liberation from a certain system of morality. We objected to the morality because it interfered with our sexual freedom. The supporters of this system claimed that it embodied the meaning—the Christian meaning, they insisted—of the world. There was one admirably simple method of confuting these people and justifying ourselves in our erotic revolt: we would deny that the world had any meaning whatever."[2]

The call today is not only for meaninglessness in life. In addition, multitudes have settled for a meaningless church where nothing is settled, and anything goes. No wonder church people are confused about social issues, and whole congregations are sidelined.

The ancient city of Corinth was a viper's nest of sexual perversion when Paul established the church there. Temple prostitutes and other sex workers were so numerous that the term "Corinthian girl" was a polite way of calling someone a whore. So how do you mitigate the radical teachings of the Bible to accommodate young people familiar with all forms of sex since they were ten years old or younger? Paul never lowered the bar. He gave them the gospel.

"Flee from sexual immorality," he warned them. "Every other sin a person commits is outside the body, but the sexually immoral person sins against his own body. Or do you not know that your body is a temple of the Holy Spirit within you, whom you have from God? You are not your own, for you were bought with a price. So glorify God in your body" (1 Cor. 6:18–20). A temple must be a dedicated space.

It's healthy and sobering to remind ourselves there's a reason we don't build temples or worship in them. That's because the body of each individual is a temple,

---

[2]Aldous Huxley, *Ends and Means: An Inquiry into the Nature of Ideals* (1937; repr., New York: Routledge, 2017), 316.

inhabited by the Holy Spirit of God. That was the promise of Christ when he said, "Whoever believes in me, as the Scripture has said, 'Out of his heart will flow rivers of living water'" (John 7:38). We can imagine how a caretaker might clean and maintain a brick-and-mortar temple, but how does one maintain a temple of flesh and blood?

Paul gives us some guidance in Ephesians 5:26–27 when he describes how Christ sanctifies the church. ". . . that he might sanctify her, having cleansed her by the washing of water with the word, so that he might present the church to himself in splendor, without spot or wrinkle or any such thing, that she might be holy and without blemish." As believers, we go the extra mile to keep our lives clean from the decay of sin and the stain of worldly lusts and ideas. No doubt, the seduction of the flesh can be powerful. Our calling is to feed our passion for Christ until it's more powerful, interwoven with the Holy Spirit's desire to exalt the Lord.

Don't miss the image of Christ mentoring the family of God here. "The one who conquers and who keeps my works until the end, to him I will give authority over the nations," he promises (Rev. 2:26). God constantly opens doors of authority and delegates roles to his disciples. We influence history and nature through our prayers. We bind broken hearts and encourage faithfulness through personal ministry. We empower broader ministry through giving. And we grow the family of God through personal evangelism. Christ assures us there's even more to come.

Then he promises to give the "morning star" to those who overcome. We don't have to guess what that might be, for Jesus explains it later in Revelation 22:16. "I am the root and the descendant of David, the bright morning star." When we present our bodies to God as living sacrifices, clean and undamaged by the world, Christ responds by giving us more of himself.

*Prayer:* Ask God to help you circumcise your heart so your allegiance is never at risk. Pray about the forms of entertainment you and your family or friends enjoy.

*Discipline:* Do a quick survey of your favorite books, TV shows, movies, websites, and events. Flag any of those you would not be able to enjoy with Christ sitting alongside you. Then confess those and uproot them from your life.

*Attitude:* "'All things are lawful for me,' but not all things are helpful. 'All things are lawful for me,' but I will not be [mastered] by anything" (1 Cor. 6:12).

## Think about It

1. Read Revelation 2:12–29. Mark or highlight the specific statements or phrases that teach the principles Christ has in mind for those churches and for us.

2. Holiness is about a path that is unique because of purpose. It's not that a follower of Christ wants to avoid the world. Rather, the believer travels differently because his heart or hers is set on very different desires and plans. How do elements of your identity in Christ keep you off the broad highway to destruction and on the narrow path to life?

3. In your own words, explain what it means to maintain your body as God's temple. How does that look in your personal life?

4. Historically, churches and denominations that surrender to the world's priorities finally decline and lose authority over time. Those who hold fast to the gospel are the ones that thrive and continue to serve. Why do you suppose that's true?

CHAPTER ELEVEN

# THE LESSONS OF SARDIS, PHILADELPHIA, AND LAODICEA

*"I know your works. You have the reputation of being alive, but you are dead. Wake up, and strengthen what remains and is about to die, for I have not found your works complete in the sight of my God."*
—Revelation 3:1–2

## Work on Your Honor, Not Your Image

Revival movements are often referred to as spiritual awakenings. For many, that sounds like large numbers of unbelievers suddenly waking up to the reality of God and the need for the gospel. In fact, mass conversions like that are merely a by-product of revival. True revival ignites when the church is awakened from spiritual death. And that's what God calls for in this letter to a church.

The congregation in Sardis has been around long enough to win a great reputation. They must have begun full of faith and vision, and surely made a measurable difference in their city. But over time things changed and priorities shifted. It seems they began to emphasize their standing in the community rather than their loyalty to the kingdom of God. That gospel heart eventually stopped beating, the definition of death.

We've all seen that sort of spiritual decline happen in present-day congregations. Historic downtown churches with massive facilities and historical résumés become weighed down with worship centers and buildings vastly larger than their vision for reaching out. Nearly everyone can point to one familiar megachurch or another that began twenty years ago with spiritual fire and numerical growth but now seems driven by corrupt theology and online virtue signaling. When the risen Savior finds a church unresponsive and disinterested in the mission, he realizes he is gazing upon a body of believers that has tragically flatlined. Resurrection is always a possibility, but that's a miracle achieved by Christ, not better use of Instagram.

In this text, Christ remembers a small segment of the church (3:4) who "have not soiled their garments" and who "walk with me in white, for they are worthy." These are the few who have continued to follow their gospel compass rather than compromising and retreating from their confession. They have insisted on integrity rather than cultural relevance. They have maintained their honor.

We can only guess how ancient pagan culture seduced the leaders at Sardis and finally captured them, but we know how it's done today. Woke culture rewards churches finding their "truth" in Jesus-plus. It's not necessary to renounce Christ entirely. Pastors and teachers who balance "offensive" biblical ideas with cultural relevance and Newthink are approved or at least tolerated until they eventually renounce their faith altogether. On the other hand, churches and leaders who stand for Christ alone and the principle of *sola scriptura* are often scorned as superstitious bigots stuck in the past. People deemed on the wrong side of history can be libeled, shunned, canceled, and even investigated by state and federal authorities.

In the letter to Sardis, "he who conquers" is the saint who maintains his integrity by remaining true to the historic call of Christ. Jesus does not call us to accept him as an advisor. The only call of the cross is Lordship: denying self and following him. And the New Testament is not a menu that allows us to select only the items we prefer. Rather, it is presented as the unique and authoritative wisdom of the God who created us and will someday judge us.

Honor requires my words and actions to align consistently with my deepest convictions. It's what Christ has in mind when he tells the parable of two sons asked by their father to go out and work in the vineyard (Matt. 21:28–31). The first son refuses, but later changes his mind and honors the request. The second son offers polite lip service but goes his own way once he's out of his father's sight. Unlike the prostitutes and tax collectors who heard John the Baptist and were changed by the Good News, many Jews in Christ's audience were immovable. "And even when you saw it, you did not afterward change your minds and believe him" (v. 32).

In the parable of the sower, Christ draws a clear distinction between the passing interest in religion and genuine faith in God. He defines good soil as "Those who, hearing the word, hold it fast in an honest and good heart, and bear fruit with patience" (Luke 8:15). He also paints a vivid picture of personal honor: honesty, a good heart, and patience in service. Honor is never swayed by the results of this week's polling or the winds of fashion.

In John's vision, Christ calls the dead church people of Sardis to wake up and conquer. One's civic reputation is nothing more than straw and stubble that will be burned up in the approach of the returning Lord. The only relevant criterion on that day will be whether or not I have honored the Savior by aligning my life with his. The fact that personal honor is so out of fashion in our secular age is just one more indication of why people of faith must recover it at all costs.

*Prayer:* Ask God to give you a pure heart and right understanding.

*Discipline:* Whenever you find yourself looking in the mirror, pondering what others might think if you said or did something, use that impulse as a trigger to ask instead what God might think of you speaking or acting in that way.

*Attitude:* "But with me it is a very small thing that I should be judged by you or by any human court. In fact, I do not even judge myself" (1 Cor. 4:3).

## Be Fearless in Doing the Right Thing

"I know your works. Behold, I have set before you an open door, which no one is able to shut. I know that you have but little power, and yet you have kept my word and have not denied my name." (Rev. 3:9)

The church at Philadelphia illustrates Paul's principle from 2 Corinthians 12:10, "For when I am weak, then I am strong." Acting upon that truth, Paul was able to take courage in the face of "weaknesses, insults, hardships, persecutions, and calamities." In a brutal age without the

sophistication of the internet or social media, being canceled was more deadly than boycotts or censorship. Yes,
it was often fatal.

The saints in Philadelphia "have little power" because
they have been gradually worn down in the face of constant hostility and persecution. Their witness for Christ
has offended powerful Jewish authorities in their city. So
rather than enjoying the brotherly love promised by the
name Philadelphia, they have endured the violent opposition often triggered by the name of Christ. Angry Jews
charge the saints have gone too far with their loyalty to a
resurrected Messiah. Intimidated pagans accuse them of
insulting their patron gods. Their refusal to bow before
Caesar, as well as Christ, is not only irreligious but threatens the foundations of the Roman Empire.

Of the seven churches singled out in Revelation, only
Philadelphia receives no criticism from the Lord. He
applauds their faith and courage in keeping his Word and
refusing to deny his name. He promises their enemies
will ultimately bow at their feet. And in the course of
seven short verses, he offers them two guarantees.

"Behold, I have set before you an open door, which
no one is able to shut" (Rev. 3:8). Their city is located
at the intersection of several major trade routes. In other
words, they won't have to battle to get the gospel to the
world. God will bring the world to them if they continue
a ministry so simple it's hard to stamp out: talking about
the Good News and loving their neighbors as themselves.
It doesn't require money or creativity to share your experience with Christ and do good to the people around
you. But when that message is considered hateful and
people like you are condemned as destructive and traitor-
ous, it does require guts.

The second guarantee is Christ will "keep you from
the hour of trial that is coming on the whole world, to try
those who dwell on the earth" (3:10). The same Greek

term meaning "to fix one's eyes upon" or "watch over"
is used twice in that verse. In more basic terms, Christ
promises "Because you fixed your eyes on my Word in
your recent trials, I will watch over you in the hour of
trial coming on the whole world." Notice, that matches
the image from Revelation 1 where John describes Jesus
standing amid the seven churches, watching over them.

One popular view of Revelation projects this historic
church into a futuristic setting, supposing this is a reference to the rapture of the church. Again, that interpretation overlooks the historical context in which John
wrote this. His original recipients in AD 90 were facing
such traumatic and terrifying persecution at the hands
of their enemies a promise to spare some future generation from a later era would have been ironic at the very
least. "We're being burned at the stake, fed to lions, and
decapitated for the name of Christ, but some disciples in
the future will get a pass? Why?" The original readers of
Revelation would have found no comfort or encouragement in the idea of God moving the goalposts, and it was
first written to them in their hour of trial.

Something powerful and eternal happens whenever
the forces of evil begin to tighten the screws in order to
stamp out faith. When royal aides and regional satraps
conspired to have Daniel thrown to the lions, their objective was to snuff out his growing influence in the Babylonian court. Ironically, God not only saved his trusted
servant but turned the tables to destroy the schemers and
astonish the king, who literally ordered his subjects to
show respect for Daniel's God (Dan. 6:26). Later in the
New Testament, Paul's ministry resulted in his arrest and
a trial before Caesar in Rome. Rather than silencing the
bold apostle, the arrest multiplied his influence. "I want
you to know, brothers, that what has happened to me has
really served to advance the gospel, so that it has become

known throughout the whole imperial guard and to all the rest that my imprisonment is for Christ" (Phil. 1:12–13). His persecution also spurred others in the church to share the gospel with greater freedom.

In AD 107, Ignatius, Bishop of Syria, was transported to Rome for trial before Emperor Trajan. If pagan Rome hoped to discourage other Christians through the bishop's mistreatment, they were bitterly disappointed. Swelling crowds thronged the roadways as Roman soldiers delivered the saint to his appointment. During the brutal journey by land and sea, the holy man wrote seven letters, warning churches to stand firm against false teachings, and asking that they not pray for his deliverance. Rather, he wanted to identify with Christ in his death. He desired his martyrdom to bear witness to the glory of God. Unlike his hero Daniel, he did not escape the teeth of the lions. Instead, he went directly into the presence of his heavenly Father, and his seven letters on the road to Rome were so widely disseminated they can still be read today, two thousand years later!

In our own century, government efforts to stamp out the Christian faith have erupted in nations large and small, but here in the United States, following Christ has seemed a mostly tranquil avocation. The 1960s saw a string of historic court rulings banning prayer and Christian principles from public schools. Strangely, those rulings were celebrated by large segments of the nation in the interest of protecting children who are too vulnerable and too immature to make reasoned decisions about faith or religion. Scarcely a generation later, the latest outcry demands that little school children must be exposed to transgender ideology and transvestite dancers. The ideas of Christ have been shut out. Small children are no longer considered vulnerable or immature, and must be allowed to demand "gender-affirming" surgery and puberty blockers. In nearly every pressing social issue, such contradictions abound.

Public opinion polling indicates Americans already button their lips on a range of issues being advanced by the government. Who wants federal agents crashing through your door at 5:00 a.m. with assault weapons and body armor? Even basic ideas like weather patterns, human biology, or childrearing are suddenly political and controversial. We have now learned even our vaunted First Amendment cannot protect us from power-hungry politicians who can impose public health emergency lockdowns, demand censorship of unpopular ideas, or stigmatize opponents as racists.

The future will require more of a resource already in short supply in this age of chaos: courage. And as a popular TV commentator recently observed, it won't be the kind of courage we have been trained to display. That is, we've known for most of our lives that any adult should have the courage to rescue a child from a burning building. That's a given. But we haven't been schooled in being brave enough to stand up in a corporate board meeting to challenge unjust ideas like the racist principle of diversity-equity-inclusion. Speaking up when it's costly and refusing to bow the knee to government overreach will demand a sort of boldness we never expected to need in polite society. But the old world of "normal" is collapsing all around us. The revolution has arrived.

Christ promises a respected place in the presence of God to anyone who dares to stand tall against the onrushing tidal wave of destruction. Like a majestic column in the temple of God, courageous saints can never be displaced or excluded. And what's more, the sacred name of God will be written across that warrior saint's life. When the Beast threatens to wreck your life and take away your good name, God promises to give you his.

*Prayer:* Ask God for the courage to live and speak the truth in love, even when it's unpopular, even when it's forbidden.

*Discipline:* As you read your Bible each day, look for verses or principles relating to pressing moral and spiritual questions of the hour. Highlight them in your Bible with a brief caption written in the margins or jot them down in a journal for future use. Think about them to retain them in your memory.

*Attitude:* "Be watchful, stand firm in the faith, act like men, be strong. Let all that you do be done in love" (1 Cor. 16:13).

## Invest in the Currency of Heaven

"For you say, I am rich, I have prospered, and I need nothing, not realizing that you are wretched, pitiable, poor, blind, and naked. I counsel you to buy from me gold refined by fire, so that you may be rich, and white garments so that you may clothe yourself and the shame of your nakedness may not be seen, and salve to anoint your eyes, so that you may see." (Rev. 3:17–18)

In his Sermon on the Mount, Christ promises his followers that we will not need to chase after money, clothing, and food the way the unbelieving world does. That's because the same God who clothes the lilies with splendor King Solomon could not rival is also willing to provide for us and equip us for life. "But seek first the kingdom of God and his righteousness," he counsels us. "And all these things will be added to you" (Matt. 6:33).

Righteousness is the currency of heaven. Take a look at these very straightforward texts:

- "And [Abraham] believed the LORD, and he counted it to him as righteousness" (Gen. 15:6).
- "Henceforth there is laid up for me the crown of righteousness, which the Lord, the righteous judge, will award to me on that day, and not only to me but also to all who have loved his appearing" (2 Tim. 4:8).
- But now the righteousness of God has been manifested apart from the law, although the Law and the Prophets bear witness to it—the righteousness of God through faith in Jesus Christ for all who believe" (Rom. 3:21–22).
- "But as for you, O man of God, flee these things. Pursue righteousness, godliness, faith, love steadfastness, gentleness. Fight the good fight of faith" (1 Tim. 6:11–12).

The New Testament describes righteousness in two different ways. Ultimate, imputed righteousness is the kind only Christ can award us. The doctrine in play here is justification: we are made right with God by grace through faith (Rom. 4:5). That transaction is what Paul has in mind when he speaks of an inheritance "that is imperishable, undefiled, and unfading, kept in heaven for you" (1 Pet. 1:4). By contrast, practical or outward righteousness begins with an appetite or an aspiration—a desire to be like Christ. What we cannot achieve through our best efforts at behavior modification, God achieves through personal transformation (2 Cor. 3:18). By faith, we leave our lives on the altar of obedience and Christ changes our attitudes first, and then our outward behavior (Rom. 12:1–2).

Unfortunately, virtues like those are out of favor in the prevailing culture of the 2020s. Today's children are most commonly taught to cultivate ambition, self-esteem, tolerance, skepticism, and love of the planet. Popular superheroes in books and movies are no longer upright men or women; they must have dark qualities or attitudes to be authentic. The mantra of this generation is "follow your heart," and righteousness is not a place the natural human heart wants to go.

The church people in Laodicea didn't want to go there either. In their minds, they were more elevated, and more complete than most people because they achieved wealth and status. Their hometown held a strategic location on key trade routes, and their banking system was respected as far away as Rome. Unfortunately, the pride that can accompany great wealth spilled over into their church.

In his letter, Jesus describes them as lukewarm and nauseating. Their blindness and corruption make him want to vomit—literally (Rev. 3:16). Although they perceive themselves as rich and lacking in nothing, Christ recognizes they are "wretched, pitiable, blind, and naked" (v. 17).

What they need most comes only from heaven. "I counsel you to buy from me gold refined by fire, so that you may be rich, and white garments so that you may clothe yourself and the shame of your nakedness may not be seen" (v. 18). The gold refined by fire is righteousness in heaven. The wealth to be desired is eternal treasure. The white garments to cover their nakedness denote righteousness.

If the sole purpose of the Christian life was to help us escape hell and arrive in heaven, perhaps we could trust Christ for riches there while indulging in the flesh here. But mere escape is not our objective. Our mission is to honor the values of the kingdom and change the flavor of the world. Hence, the fruit that God's Spirit comes to cultivate within us includes love, joy, peace, patience, kindness, goodness, gentleness, and self-control (Gal. 5:22–23).

God desires spiritual warriors who are also good men and women, people who treat others with kindness and hunger for righteousness. In 1 Corinthians 9, Paul likens himself to an Olympic runner, explaining how he strictly disciplines his body to keep it under control, lest he be disqualified. Like Paul, we impose rugged discipline upon ourselves while showing grace and mercy to others. Our world is well-stocked with narcissists, tyrants, manipulators, and ruthless people who want to be rich. The salt this foul culture needs is faith leading to righteousness.

Concluding his rebuke of the Laodiceans, Christ advises them that he continues to knock on the door, hoping they will let him in. To the one who overcomes and invites him in, he promises fellowship with him and the privilege of sharing his throne. "The one who conquers, I will grant him to sit with me on my throne, as I also conquered and sat down with my Father on his throne" (Rev. 3:21).

*Prayer:* Ask God daily for the wisdom to make the kinds of decisions and engage in the kinds of deeds that bear interest in heaven, not simply praise or rewards on earth.

*Discipline:* Examine your life for instances where you have excused sin and disobedience because of a particular situation. In those moments, you were linking your righteousness to some factor other than Christ. Commit yourself to righteousness and personal conduct that rests on Christ alone.

*Attitude:* "Do not be conformed to this world, but be transformed by the renewal of your mind, that by testing you may discern what is the will of God, what is good and acceptable and perfect" (Rom. 12:2).

## Think about It

1. Read Revelation 3. Mark or highlight specific statements or phrases that convey the lessons for these three churches and for us as well.
2. How many of your neighbors or coworkers know Jesus is Lord in your life? Do you think it's important to Christ for people familiar with your most basic life facts to know about your faith? Why or why not?
3. Think of a time or incident when your faith called you to do something bold and courageous. If you can't recall a moment like that, can you still remember a time when you should have been brave but were not?
4. How would you explain the way wealth can blind us to our deepest needs and our true, spiritual condition?

# CHAPTER TWELVE

# THIS PRESENT DARKNESS

*Here is a call for the endurance and faith of the saints.*
—Revelation 13:10

These are not normal times. One of the questions raised most frequently by ordinary Americans on all sides of the political divide is "What happened? How did things spiral into madness so suddenly?"

After decades of championing the free exchange of ideas, the largest news organizations in the country started demanding censorship and the suppression of speech because they regard so many opinions as dangerous. Intellectuals and policymakers insist with straight faces that men can have babies. After the October 7, 2023, slaughter of 1,200 Israeli civilians by invaders from Hamas, the hatred of Jews has become fashionable across college campuses and in the media, both here and abroad. And in large cities across the United States, serious crimes like theft, robbery, carjacking, rape, and even murder are no longer punished because criminals are a victim class. Worst of all, speaking out against such preposterous notions is not only discouraged but can be punished severely.

When a government assumes the power to impose one viewpoint upon every political question, *and when every issue is suddenly political,* it means the Beast is on the rise. This is bigger than politics because a takeover so sweeping requires participation at some level from both sides of the aisle. And it's not recent. The direction of our nation's drift from God has been set for more than sixty years. Elections come and go, but the heart of darkness underlying our political system is immune to the influence of voters, legislation, or even investigations. Ours is a spiritual struggle, the kind that always results in hostility toward Christians, hatred of Jews, and finally persecution.

At the moment, Catholics are under fire for their strong stand against abortion, and the term *evangelical* has become synonymous with Neanderthal. Jews were above the fray for a while, but they have recently been shocked to discover the popular Holocaust museums and the promise "Never Forget" have failed to persuade many. Now we hear calls for genocide against the Jews on college campuses are not necessarily a form of harassment. The social turbulence in this country will only intensify, not unlike the hostility and violence spreading among nations around the globe. It's a painful reminder that we don't belong here but are merely deployed for a while on assignment from heaven.

Jesus of Nazareth lived in the kingdom of God every single day he walked the rocky terrain of Israel. He faced a profound undertaking with a short, urgent timeline, yet he never seemed rushed or anxious. There was time to find Zacchaeus perched in a tree and invite him to lunch, to wait by a well for the woman from Samaria. Charged with literally changing the course of the world, he poured most of his time into twelve ordinary men, and never left the borders of his tiny homeland. He lived his entire life from an eternal perspective.

He was never seduced to soften the message because of his approaching zero hour. He never faltered in his mission, even when powerful forces threatened to destroy him. Jesus remained faithful to his father's calling, despite all the temptations to try something different. And he left us a rich, enduring legacy.

That's a powerful character trait, *endurance*. The term is employed five times in John's Revelation, always regarding the saints. Situations call for endurance. We are commanded to endure. Some are rewarded for enduring. Then there's that other word, *perseverance*, used three times in Revelation, always concerning the people of God. The Greek term for *patience* shows up four times. Doing the right thing is never easy and rarely popular. Followers of Jesus Christ carry a cross every day, and there's no shortcut to eternity.

We should unburden ourselves of the fantasy that our victory must come soon. The early church grew in number, leaped across borders, and took root in distant cultures at a rate we've never seen since. Still, the scattered persecution of Christians continued in the Roman Empire until Emperor Constantine became a believer in AD 312. Believers in China have heroically battled the Beast since 1949. The losses have been heavy, but the church has continued to multiply and bear witness. The lessons of history tell us we must be patient and plan for the long haul, not for some temporary inconvenience before things rebound quickly to normal.

Election seasons are important because elections have consequences, and wise citizens should always vote. But we aren't electing a savior, and election results are a Band-Aid at best. Only Christ can address the heart issues underlying the spiritual warfare raging in the West today. Politics are now so polarized the best policies of one administration can be completely reversed by the next. Of course, the faith remedy offered by God has always been heart change, not regime change. Church people who pin their hopes on a political agenda rather than the kingdom of God will always be disappointed by the next court decision or the next election.

As much as some prefer the sprint, spiritual warfare is a marathon. We are rarely able to draw a straight line from cause to eternal impact for there's often a generation or even a century in between. Faith steels long-suffering saints with a long view of eternity and progress. By faith, let's rejoin John on Patmos once again to rehearse how we become overcomers.

## Love by Faith. Selflessly. Tirelessly. Sacrificially.

Read the signs of the times and you'll realize there's no more time for the sort of petty wrangling and sniping sometimes marking church life in the United States. Allowing trifling differences to escalate into public rancor and division has always been un-Christlike and unloving. But with the approach of the all-consuming evil God calls "the Beast," the failure to unite and stand is madness.

As European pioneers advanced across the American West in the 1800s, a clash of empires with the Indians was inevitable. One can speculate about how the native Americans were never positioned to succeed against the numbers, the contagious viruses, the financial resources, or the weapons technology bearing down upon them. But it is a fact that the various tribes always felt more threatened by each other than they did by the foreign invasion. They never managed to unite. The cavalry was always able to enlist one tribe to serve as spies and guides to help them attack other tribes. When the Civil War finally summoned all the soldiers and fighters away from the frontier and back to conflicts in the East, the Indians used the break in hostilities to resume old skirmishes and settle scores against neighboring tribes. Their destruction became a certainty.

Whoever has ears should hear this: it's past time for the saints to love each other faithfully and unite around Jesus Christ.

## Choose a Good Death Over a Craven Life

One of the most instructive moments in the New Testament is found in Acts 4 when Peter and John are arrested for preaching about the resurrection. After being locked away overnight in hopes their passion will cool, the two are dragged before the rulers and the elders who warn them to stop talking about Jesus. Unshaken, the two men reply, "Whether it is right in the sight of God to listen to you rather than to God, you must judge, for we cannot but speak of what we have seen and heard." Warned a second time, the two apostles are released to rejoin their fellow believers. They recount the events of the day, before calling the entire group to prayer. And what a prayer! They don't give in to fear and uncertainty. They refuse to be ruled by their emotions. Instead, they surrender to the power and purposes of Christ.

Here's the conclusion of their cry to the Lord. "And now, Lord, look upon their threats and grant to your servants to continue to speak your word with all boldness" (Acts 4:29). After their prayer, the room is shaken, and they are all filled anew with the Holy Spirit! As a result, they continue to defy the speech police and boldly share the Good News.

The same people who have told us for decades the world is overpopulated are now strategizing how to "save lives" in the next pandemic, Disease X. You can be sure another epidemic of "emergency measures" is in the works, but followers of Christ can no longer be caught unawares. The Beast never lets a crisis go to waste, but we must never let an opportunity be turned against us. Any future epidemic can afford us a moment when believers can rise to the occasion and demonstrate sacrificial love and supernatural faith. We can live boldly and care for our neighbors. We can share medicines and deliver food to the sick. We can offer hope through prayer and corporate worship. And we can resist the schemes of the Beast by speaking truth to unchecked power. Politicians may debate which protocols they should follow, but we have no choice but to follow Christ.

Whoever has ears should hear this: We have been buried with Christ and raised to walk in newness of life. We are not afraid of death.

## Be Holy. Stop Trying to Be Relevant

Holiness means God's purposes are my pathway. We must be like those NFL players who insist football is how they make their living, but God is whom they serve. Far more than any vices we avoid, it's the things we do that demonstrate our allegiance and our priorities.

A few years ago, a pastor's conference in Colorado Springs invited the mayor to speak at one of their regular meetings. He was invited to challenge them with some shiny, new project they might jointly undertake to positively impact the city. To their astonishment, he advised them they should teach their people to love their neighbors. The city lacked personnel and resources to address all the personal trials of a vast population, but their church members were already living among those vulnerable individuals, often right next door.

The pastors were embarrassed that a political figure had to show up at a meeting to remind Christian leaders of Christ's most basic command: love your neighbor as yourself. Do you suspect that reminder still needs to reach a lot of churches and believers today? Our neighbors are more depressed, frustrated, worried, and isolated than they've been in decades. They don't want to know how frequently we worship or which translation of the Bible we read, but they would be glad to see how much we care because our Master cares. Holiness starts in my home and then spills over to my neighbors.

Whoever has ears, should hear this: Jesus never needed the approval of powerful people or the fashionable few. Why should you?

## Your Body Is God's Temple. Dedicate It

In one of his most memorable texts, Paul makes a revealing statement about personal worship. First, he urges us to present our bodies "as a living sacrifice, holy and acceptable to God." When he continues, warning us not to be like everyone else in the world, he motivates us to "be transformed by the renewal of your mind, that by testing you may discern what is the will of God, what is good and acceptable and perfect" (Rom. 12:1–2). If your body is a temple of God, your brain is surely the Most Holy Place, the altar where dedication takes place.

The mind must be constantly renewed because life is mercurial, ever morphing and spinning off new temptations and fresh challenges. The Greek word translated as "renewal" comes from a root meaning "to grow up." Two primary measures of maturity are the criteria we use for making choices and the judgment we demonstrate in applying them wisely. In fact, teaching healthy discrimination is the motive behind many of those curious laws in the Old Testament: don't mix wool and linen or plant your vineyard with two different seeds. God knew broken people escaping a lifetime of bondage needed coaching to draw healthy distinctions for themselves. So, he instructed them, not so differently from the way we teach toddlers to recognize different shapes.

Keep the nerve center of your temple armed with ideas, principles, and stories from God's Word. The Holy Spirit brings these truths to combustion, keeping the fire in your heart burning fiercely. This energizes your mind so you can draw clear distinctions and be decisive. Vague decisions leave you susceptible to temptation and missing the mark. In Romans 13:14, Paul addresses that hazard. Advising saints to walk in the sunlight, far away from sexual immorality and sensuality, he cautions us, "But put on the Lord Jesus Christ, and make no provision for the flesh, to gratify its desires." Quite literally, we are counseled to walk within the guidance of Christ and never make decisions so vague or flexible that they leave an opening for caving to sin.

The Beast wants more than your taxes and your obedience to some basic laws. Absolute control demands he must reduce you to a mere cipher by telling you how to think, what to believe, and how to stay on the right side of history. The best way to combat that is with biblical convictions and clear thinking. Caesar can lay claim to your taxes, but your mind and body belong to God.

Whoever has ears should hear this: The way you worship is shaped by the way you think. Never trade away your right to think biblically.

# Work on Your Honor, Not Your Image

On the night of Christ's arrest, his lawless trial runs late into the evening without much success. There's no doubt the scurrilous witnesses are lying. Their accusations are so shallow and meritless they must have been paid to bear false witness. Two men finally agree Jesus spoke of destroying the temple in three days, but that's such an unlikely feat it doesn't get much credence. So it's with no small amount of desperation that Caiaphas, the high priest, finally turns to Jesus. "I adjure you by the living God, tell us if you are the Christ, the Son of God" (Matt. 26:63).

To adjure is to demand that someone must answer under oath. Christ has just been ordered to divulge if he really is the Christ, the Son of God—and to do so under oath. One simple lie can save him a lot of grief. Why should he say anything to advance this kangaroo court proceeding? Why? Because the Messiah has come to bear witness to the truth. Telling a lie—even an untruth that might thwart injustice—is not an option. Besides, he's under oath.

"You have said so," Christ replies. "But I tell you, from now on you will see the Son of Man seated at the right hand of Power and coming on the clouds of heaven" (v. 64). It's a glorious truth. At this particular moment, it's also a painful one leading to a deadly afternoon on an agonizing cross. But as the wheels of eternity continue to turn, the truth will bring glory to Christ and set millions free.

Life in Christ means you and I are based and rooted in truth. Our mission requires we always speak the truth and never lie. We are commanded, "Let what you say be simply 'Yes' or 'No'; anything more than this comes from evil" (Matt. 5:37). It's a simple statement but a demanding discipline: never playing with words, shading the facts, or blurring the message. No timely silence, giving the impression we are in step with the mob.

The woke voices of our culture never mince their words in dictating what we ought to believe. Their shameful values are constantly advanced in entertainment and media, in bureaucratic policies, and even in private conversations. Most often, Christians cough nervously or look away as neighbors and coworkers spout the slogans of Newthink, never wondering who might disagree or even be offended. Only when the people of God man up and speak the truth in love can we finally commence that long-awaited national conversation. Don't try to blend in. Bring Jesus to the party.

Whoever has ears should hear this: integrity can be costly, but that's because it's precious.

## Be Fearless in Doing the Right Thing

Aleksandr Solzhenitsyn faced the Beast in his own generation in the Soviet Union. Condemned for anti-government activities in 1945, he spent a decade in work camps, political gulags, and finally in exile. Early on he was an unbeliever but still refused to bow to the demands of atheistic tyrants. Years of deprivation stripped away all his personal atheistic illusions, allowing him to recognize the splendor of Jesus Christ and the essential nature of the gospel in maintaining a civilized society. He later wrote, "The simple step of a courageous individual is not to take part in the lie. One word of truth outweighs the world."

Faith is complete reliance on God who empowers us to embrace towering truths and do hard things. No doubt, you have already discovered in your own life how faith grows through exercise. The more you trust, the more you learn to trust.

Inviting your friends and relatives to trust Jesus Christ can be intimidating if you've never done it. You feel inadequate. People can be so prickly about spiritual matters. It seems impossible to build a bridge from trivial conversations to something as serious as faith. That's true but driving a car can be terrifying to teenagers trying it for the first time. *How will I ever keep this vehicle between those narrow white lines?* And yet, as every parent knows, that lack of confidence evaporates quickly with a bit of experience. Sharing your faith is not that different. After a few practice runs, you can do it, sometimes without thinking.

Raising your children to trust God and cultivate a spiritual life can also seem impossible. The world constantly undermines you. Video games and new friends are far more interesting than character-building. The whole enterprise seems so intensive and complicated that you wonder where you even start. It's not where, but when. If you have children, you start today by simply talking about your own experiences with God and ideas you've gained from Scripture even in routine conversations. You start wherever you are: driving them to school, helping them clean their room, sharing a pizza with them. It may be slightly awkward, but don't all the important conversations with immature children feel that way? Unlike driving or sharing your faith, it doesn't necessarily get easier with experience, but it becomes much more satisfying as you see discipline beginning to grow.

The world says you're a victim: you need a helping hand from the government. Faith says, "Finally, be strong in the Lord and in the strength of his might" (Eph. 6:10). Don't get caught in the web of lies being spun all around you. Stop looking for safe spaces and join Jesus Christ in the adventure of your life.

Whoever has ears should hear this: Confidence comes from learning to do the things that frighten you. Strap on your parachute and jump.

## Invest in the Currency of Heaven

Righteousness is both a treasure stored up for us in heaven and an ambition to walk like Jesus here on earth. Both dynamics are captured in generous living. When we see ourselves as rivers of blessing rather than reservoirs, we look more like Christ in the eyes of others, and we begin to accrue interest in Eternity.

Returning a tithe, one-tenth, to the local church is another of those hard things faith calls us to do. Some pastors are reluctant to preach about generosity because it seems like a very sensitive topic. Frankly, the idea of giving away blessings is only touchy for people who already feel guilty and don't understand how satisfying it is. The rest of us have discovered living with open hands brings a lot of joy, not only to the ones who receive help but also to the ones privileged to be instruments of God.

Like the emperors who promised bread and circuses to distract the Roman people from all the graft and corruption, our own politicians constantly brainstorm new benefits to offer the poor suckers. Never mind the nine most terrifying words in the English language are "I'm from the government and I'm here to help." Moreover, it's been demonstrated time and again that Christian NGOs are more efficient and even more timely in helping victims of disaster. Churches are more effective in cultivating supportive community than federal bureaucrats. And generous neighbors are far more personal and caring than nameless government agents fidgeting behind intimidating desks, loaded down with forms to sign and memos to draft.

When Paul assures the saints "whoever sows bountifully will reap bountifully," he employs figurative language to illustrate a literal truth (2 Cor. 9:6). Growth of ministry follows growth in generosity, but profound, personal blessings surprise us as well. God has promised he will enrich us so we can be even more capable of spreading the blessings around. Trust him wholeheartedly and see where it leads.

Whoever has ears should hear this: your savings account in heaven is easily neglected, but one day it's all that will matter.

## Eternity and the Next Three Hundred Years

There's a reason they call it breaking news. The latest outrage from fifteen minutes ago can break your concentration and send you into a panic. Headline hype about another political catastrophe in the works for tomorrow can shatter your peace of mind. Revelation reminds us the kingdom of God is still on track, unflustered by so much human folly under the sun. Timeless perspective can be yours and mine, as well.

My favorite cathedral in all the world is York Minster, an awe-inspiring edifice in the United Kingdom, completed in 1472. Magnificent stained-glass windows tell the stories of the Bible. Arches and altars point the worshipper to the Most High God of heaven and earth. Everything about this enduring cathedral urges us to fall in awe and gratitude. My wife and I were able to worship there one evening in a service we will never forget.

It must have taken more than three centuries to complete this building project. From the outset, everyone knew it would be costly and time-consuming, and the men and women who first devoted themselves to this labor of love realized they would not live long enough to walk inside and worship there. It would not be finished in their children's lifetimes either. Still, they labored and gave, and prayed.

Why take on such a task? They did it because Jesus Christ is worthy of something costly, majestic, and extraordinary. They did it to display the power and the promise of what awaits us in eternity. And they did it for posterity: for grandchildren, great-grandchildren, and the people of tomorrow.

This is why we join in the struggle of our generation, a war that may well outlast us and rage for a hundred years unless the Lord returns sooner. We do it because Jesus is worthy. We do it because eternity awaits with all the glory of God. And we do it for posterity and the children of the future.

I hope you'll offer up a prayer like this with me, today and often.

> *Heavenly Father, may your name be hallowed; may your will be done in my life as it is in your kingdom; instantly and completely. Lord, give me the love to walk patiently with your people and see your kingdom advance across the earth. Please give me the faith to live boldly, even if it should cost me everything. And please give me the hope to hold on until the end, trusting you to make my offering matter. Let my life honor the name of Jesus Christ. Amen.*

## Think about It

And I heard a voice from heaven saying, "Write this: Blessed are the dead who die in the Lord from now on." "Blessed indeed," says the Spirit, "that they may rest from their labors, for their deeds follow them!" (Rev. 14:13)

1. Read Revelation 14:13 again. As the camp of the saints, when do we rest from our labors? What does it mean that our deeds will follow us?
2. The recurring theme of the New Testament is we should prepare for the return of Christ, even though we can never know when it will happen. How could it benefit us to anticipate the Lord's return and think about it often?
3. What should be our response to a world that seems largely disinterested in the gospel of Jesus Christ?
4. Many parents feel they don't have the time or know-how to personally train up godly sons and daughters. What's the starting point for godly parenting? How can moms and dads gain confidence?
5. Commit to read through Revelation in entirety one chapter at a time over the next month. Don't try to solve every mystery in the first run-through. Rather, ask questions like these:

   - What do the major images represent?
   - What do the numbers mentioned here suggest?
   - Is there a spiritual truth here I can identify and think about?

The Battle: Tactics for
Biblical Manhood Learned
from the 7th Cavalry in Vietnam

Paperback 9781735428567/
eBook 9781735428574

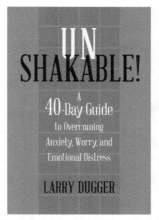

Unshakable!: A 40-Day Guide
to Overcoming Anxiety,
Worry, and Emotional Distress

Paperback 9781735856384/
eBook 9781735856391

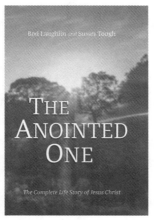

The Anointed One: The Complete Life Story of Jesus Christ

Hardcover 9781956454345/
eBook 9781956454352

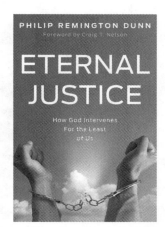

Eternal Justice: How God Intervenes for the Least of Us

Paperback 9781736620625/ eBook 9781736620632

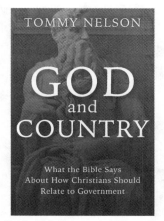

God and Country: What the Bible Says About How Christians Should Relate to Government

Hardcover 9781956454284/ eBook 9781956454291

Strong and Courageous: A Call to Biblical Manhood

Paperback 9781736620687/ eBook 9781736620694